A HISTORY OF MUSIC
IN PICTURES

EDITED BY
GEORG KINSKY

WITH THE CO-OPERATION OF
ROBERT HAAS, HANS SCHNOOR
AND OTHER EXPERTS

WITH AN INTRODUCTION
BY
ERIC BLOM

NEW YORK
E. P. DUTTON & CO. INC.

FOREWORD

THE awakening, in the nineteenth century, of the historical sense under the stimulus of such far-sighted thinkers as Herder and Winckelmann prepared the way at the same time for a scientific account of the development of music. The task which confronts music historians of to-day is that of fitting art facts into their right place within the broad framework of intellectual and cultural linkages. In view of its purely scientific basis, music history has become recognized as an independent branch of pedagogy and research, and is now aspiring, with encouraging results, to the position long held by the histories of its sister arts. A large force of professional workers is engaged on its problems, foremost of which at the moment is the key inquiry into the nature and significance of musical style. The profusion of problems, alien to modern feeling, which arises in this connexion may account for the slight interest taken by amateurs in general in the results of musical research — notwithstanding the recent successful co-operation between workers and performers in attempts to revive the still neglected treasures of the past and introduce them to the present as the stimulating elements of a new renaissance.

A similar attempt is made, by the publication of this book, to stimulate the revival of music history for pleasure and profit. The intention is to mirror its course throughout the centuries and present the reflections to our readers 'in pictures,' although we realize that pictorial representations can be but make-shifts in visualizing the growth of an art of sound of a different variety from our own. Yet pictorial representations are in many cases the only aids to an insight into the musical life and activity of bygone times; apart from some unimportant exceptions they are indeed the only proofs left to us which still reflect the flourishing musical culture of antiquity, now long since vanished, and a great part of the medieval. These pictures alone can give us a conception of that which modern renderings fail to give, or give imperfectly. They alone can supplement and strengthen our slender knowledge of the actual music of former times. In the monuments erected to music by the sculptor's art; in the illumination and notation of old manuscripts; in the portrayal of the singers, of instruments, and those who play them, we see revealed the face and stamp of the age, the spirit of an environment to which in due time the greatest creative minds rose superior. But the nearer we come to the favoured age of the Renaissance and the threshold of modern times — the dawn of the *nuove musiche*, of monody — the more extensive and varied becomes the field of vision, amplified and rounded off as it is by portraits and autographs of famous composers, by specimens of printed music and a survey of the families of instruments. In the baroque period the new art-form of opera claims a substantial place in the narrative, while from the eighteenth century onward — the age of classicism — biographical examples predominate, and the creations of painter and sculptor fall somewhat into the background.

That this is emphatically no mere picture book, however, is evident from the whole layout of the work, which is designed as a source of inspiration and instruction to every serious music-lover and also as a supplement — in respect of its living outlook — to every book on music history, whether scientific or popular. It embraces a space of four thousand five hundred years; the series of illustrations begins with sculptures from Asia dating from the middle of the third millennium B.C. and closes with portraits of the pioneers of Impressionism. The limitations imposed by the single handy volume form necessitated a severe sifting of the mass of material, amounting to some 2,500 illustrations, which was the outcome of years of diligent research.   In making the selection the centre of gravity was deliberately placed in earlier times — up to the seventeenth century inclusive — since the pictorial material of later times is sufficiently familiar and easily available in such a work as, for instance, Gustav Kanth's *Bilder-Atlas zur Musikgeschichte von Bach bis Strauss* (Berlin, 1911).   This applies particularly to the nineteenth century, which is dealt with purely as a cross-section containing specimens of outstanding names.   The music of the present day has been excluded — and that not for considerations of space alone.   Its foundation is placed at about the year 1910 and portraits are given of Strauss, Mahler, Reger, Busoni, and Debussy: master composers whose names have in the meantime become 'historical.'

The editor and the publishers of the book have met with liberal and willing assistance both at home and abroad: the directors of a large number of museums, picture galleries, libraries, archives, and publishing houses, and the owners of private collections, have displayed a gratifying interest in the undertaking, thus rendering its publication possible.   At the head of the list must be placed the music departments of the Prussian Staatsbibliothek, Berlin (Prof. Dr. Wilhelm Altmann and Johannes Wolf), the British Museum, London (the late W. Barclay Squire), and the Nationalbibliothek, Vienna (Prof. Dr. Robert Haas).   We have further to thank the Liceo Musicale di Bologna (Francesco Vatielli), the former Heyer collection of instruments at the Musikwissenschaftliche Institut, Leipzig (Prof. Dr. Theodor Kroyer), and the museum of the Gesellschaft der Musikfreunde, Vienna (the late Prof. Dr. Eusebius Mandyczevski).   The treasures assembled for the Frankfurt Exhibition of 1927 ('Musik im Leben der Völker') also yielded valuable booty. The whole of the editing and classification of material was in the hands of the undersigned, who was assisted by a number of well-known experts, through whose untiring zeal the illustrations for individual sections of the book were obtained: Gerald Cooper, London (*England*); Prof. Dr. Robert Haas, Vienna (*Notation and Opera*); Dr. Emil Kunze, Athens (*Antiquity*); Henry Prunières, Paris (*France*); J. B. Trend, London (*Spain*); and Dr. Heinz Zirnbauer, Munich (*Medieval Miniatures*).   The editor's sincere thanks are due to these and the many helpers who remain anonymous, as well as to his friend Dr. Hans Schnoor of Dresden, who drew up the preliminary schemes, and to two young student colleagues who rendered service by obtaining pictures and preparing the work for the press: Erhard Göpel (*cand. phil.*), of Leipzig, and Walter Schürenberg, of München-Gladbach.

GEORG KINSKY

Cologne, Summer 1929.

INTRODUCTION

ICONOGRAPHY is a neglected branch of musical science. Those who have brought out an illustrated book on any musical subject can tell a tale of research and labour compared with which the writing of the text itself was a holiday task. Despite the unfailing courtesy and helpfulness encountered at libraries, museums, and art galleries, a musical writer could scarcely become engaged in a more exhausting process than that of elucidating a given subject by a set of pictures, while the search after some particular illustration too often proves altogether baffling. The almost limitless collection of books on music in the British Museum is readily accessible through the catalogue and the subject-index, but illustrations in these books, which might be an invaluable aid to musical research, are frequently brought to light only by a fortunate accident. The admirable print room at the same institution is even more interesting to an author from the iconographical point of view because much of the material stored there has never been reproduced in books; but although the collection is a treasure house, the fact that it has not so far been catalogued renders it less useful than it might be. To give only two instances. How many musicians are aware that a recently discovered portrait of Orlandus Lassus is reproduced in Adolf Sandberger's *Ausgewählte Aufsätze zur Musikgeschichte*? Who can tell whether there is not an unknown likeness of Handel on some engraving safely stored under 'London Coffee Houses' or 'Tavern Scenes of the Eighteenth Century'?

There are, further, useful pictures in our art collections, such as those of the two ladies at the virginals by Vermeer in the National Gallery, Jan Steen's 'Harpsichord Lesson' and 'Lute Player' in the Wallace Collection, and many other equally valuable pictorial aids to the study of old instruments. Again, we have the instruments themselves at the Victoria and Albert Museum, the Royal College of Music, and elsewhere. Thus it is in London; thus it is, multiplied a thousandfold, in all the places in Europe and beyond where art and art documents are stored.

The writer on music may be told that it is part of his business, and not the least fascinating part after all, to undertake research of this sort. Well and good; but what of those for whom the study of musical matters can only be a diversion? There are such people — perhaps as many to-day as ever — and nobody who displays any sort of interest in music is more deserving than they of professional assistance. They cannot wander from pillar to post every time they wish to see an instrument or a print or a portrait that might remove a doubt or settle a point of dispute, and they have no time for elaborate investigations. Neither, for that matter, has the executive professional musician.

It is not now beyond all probability that a central public music library will one day be established here, and it is hoped that one of the important features of such an institution will be a complete iconographical index referring to prints and book illustrations to be found in the collection. This has in fact already made some progress, but must necessarily remain in private hands until the opportunity comes to realize the ultimate aim to make it public property. It should one day become possible to see portraits of any musician, pictures of any instrument, and pictorial representations of all sorts of musico-historical events at a moment's notice. Even so, however, the student and the lover of music will only be able to peer into this or that corner of musical history: they will not, except with some trouble, have a pictorial survey of that history as a whole.

The present book offers such a survey almost literally at a glance. It is not a history so much as an aid to history, for it presents facts without explaining them, except by the briefest of notes. That is not to say that it fails to elucidate them, for although it does not expound them verbally, it immediately stimulates the beholder's imagination and so replaces the narrative of an event or the description of some instrument and the music played on it by another kind of information which, where the object of inquiry is more important as an art than as a science, is at least as trustworthy as that furnished by the chronicler and the critic. The sight of a portrait of Matthew Locke or Hasse or Rameau tells us nothing about their music if we are not acquainted with it already; but if we know only a little, it is curious to find how much more definitely it seems to take its place in the whole trend of the art, once we have come face to face with the composer. His outward appearance somehow adds to our understanding of what his music tells us of its period, while the expression of his face, once retained by the memory, goes far towards dispelling the notion, too easily conceived through hearing alone, that one old composer's work is very much of a piece with that of all his contemporaries. There may be no resemblance between his features and those of his music — we must in fact beware of seeking it — but once an auditive impression has been strengthened by a visual one, it is much more likely to remain. A composer's autograph has almost as strong an associative effect. One need be no graphologist to see in a signature or in a manuscript music page something of a man's character and, it follows, the character of his work.

For the study of musical instruments, without which the study of music itself is fraught with countless obscurities and confusions, this book will henceforth be one of the important sources. Never, surely, have so many illustrations been assembled to give us an insight into the appearance and use of obsolete instruments. Especially commendable is the extent of the collection of pictures showing this or that instrument actually played. In many cases we almost seem to hear what kind of music was performed on these forgotten contrivances: the look or the attitude of the player is often astonishingly evocative. Can we doubt, on seeing the Ghent altar-piece by the van Eycks (p. 56), that the music of the time — these angels might be singing Binchois or Dufay or Dunstable — which now seems so frigid to us on paper, has intense emotional expression? Must not several pictures of figures playing in consort music of an obviously sacred character (as on p. 53, for example) lead us to the conclusion that early church music was by no means so exclusively vocal as we are taught to believe, though the instruments must have merely doubled vocal parts or may in some cases have been employed to play them alone? Again, the picture of an angel playing the hurdy-gurdy (organistrum, p. 58, 2) tells us some interesting things: it shows that this instrument once had a dignity it lost later, if not that religious music in and before the fifteenth century was not always as dignified as we imagine. The latter view is confirmed also by the 'angel concerts' (p. 70 has a good example). If angels could be imagined to play bagpipes and tambourines and cymbals, human beings too must have used them in their devotions. Two things of vast importance to our knowledge of this period are attested by pictures, things which musical history that takes its records from written documents tells us but vaguely: there was no gulf between sacred and secular music, and though no instrumental music is preserved, it was evidently widely practised, both extemporaneously and in the form of accompaniment to vocal music. In short, where knowledge fails us, conjecture is often so stimulated by this picture book as to give us of itself a new insight into many phases of musical evolution. The work does not appear before us laden with erudition, though much has gone to its making; but nobody will look through it without feeling that information is acquired or, if one likes to fancy that there is none left to acquire, consolidated and clarified.

.   .   .   .   .   .

Up to the Middle Ages — let us say the time of Hucbald of St. Amand, which is duly dealt with — the results of this book are those of archaeological rather than musicological research. We know so little about the music that was played on the instruments shown on the first thirty pages or so, that it was merely a question of obtaining as much representative material as could be found in various museums and collections and letting it speak for itself as best it can.   It tells us, in the nature of things, a little more at any rate about instrumental than about vocal music.   Tradition has it that all music up to the invention of the organum, or diaphony, was entirely non-harmonic, which is far easier to accept from a narrative history than from pictorial evidence.   Is it possible, we cannot help asking, that all those assemblies of instruments seen on Assyrian sculptures, on Egyptian mural paintings, in Greek plastic art, invariably played in unison? Were two harp strings really never struck simultaneously and were the two pipes of the Greek aulos always played in unison or in alternation, difficult though it must have been to avoid blowing two different notes at once?   Was it not inevitable that some sort of harmony should occasionally be produced, even if only by accident, and must not such accidents, if nothing else, have led to the discovery of harmony long before the period at which musical history places it?

The gap between the Roman age (p. 21) and the eighth century — (p. 31 would have been better placed before p. 30) — must not be regarded as strictly chronologically bridged by the eight pages devoted to the East.   Oriental instruments, owing to the tenacious conservatism which has preserved them, and their music, unaltered for many centuries, cannot with any degree of certainty be placed in the time of their origin.   Thus eighteenth-century Japanese woodcuts (p. 25) do not show typical eighteenth-century instruments, but instruments of considerable antiquity still in use at that time.   Modern Japanese pictures, which incidentally would exhibit a similar traditionalism in graphic art by displaying very much the same style of representation, would show them still in use to-day.

There are plenty of good reasons, then, for the omissions and for the somewhat uncertain chronology in these early pages, reasons quite independent of musico-historical scholarship.   Neither need the compiler's learning be called in question during the perusal of the subsequent pages, which in fact give more than enough evidence of it.   There is always the possibility to be borne in mind that certain phases had perforce to be left unrepresented for lack of material.   The author is no doubt well aware that the first exponents of the *ars nova* in France were Philippe de Vitry and Guillaume de Machaut in the fourteenth century, though in his book we do not come upon French music (as distinct from instruments) until the fifteenth century.   Probably there are no portraits of these two masters preserved, while the MSS. by Machaut in the Bibliothèque Nationale and the Marquis de Vogüé's collection as well as Vitry's treatises may be either inaccessible or pictorially uninteresting.

If one considers that this work is produced in the country that cultivates music most widely to-day, one cannot but specially commend the fact that it shows no particular national bias.   If for some periods German pictures seem to have been a little too extensively drawn upon, this is felt to be due to the greater accessibility of material rather than to any wish to emphasize a pre-eminence in music that does not date very far back.   A natural tendency to go to the nearest source is especially noticeable where we come upon the engravings of Italian opera in Germany, which cover no less than five pages (pp. 182–6).   It is true that they are more than delightful, but would it not have been possible to obtain equally charming prints of Italian opera in Italy?

   ·   ·   ·   ·   ·   ·

I cannot refrain from drawing attention to the remarkable way in which the enormous difficulty of naming the instruments on the old pictures has been met.   Even were one able to claim a knowledge equal to that revealed by those who are responsible for the work, one would scarcely detect a single mistake.   It may perhaps be questioned whether the *flûtes à bec* on pp. 244–5 ought not to have been called *Bockflöten* in the German edition, in which case the English translator would doubtless have called them 'recorders.' Apart from this, the only evasion that seems to have been committed in the descriptions of the older pictures is that of calling many of the bowed string instruments simply *Fiedeln* in German, which the translator renders, quite faithfully but equally vaguely, by 'fiddles.'   A fiddle may be all sorts of things, and to use the name for any instrument in a work such as this is rather like describing some of the illustrations in a book on ornithology as those of 'birds.' Many of these instruments are undoubtedly rebecs, but others may be *viole da braccio, lire da braccio, gigues*, bowed *vihuelas*, or what not. I confess that I would not myself take the responsibility of naming them all.

Here again there is infinitely more to admire than to question. The obscure and often very primitively reproduced instruments shown on the earlier pages are generally labelled with a certainty that is astonishing. Musical research before the time of Notker Balbulus and Hucbald is so entangled with ethnography and archaeology as to exasperate the musician who is anxious to know something of the aesthetics of his art in its infancy almost as much as it interests him. It is obvious that these two sciences have been well applied to the section dealing with antiquity and with the East. About the actual nature of music we get nothing from these pages but the vaguest suggestions; still, they are rather less indefinite than those found in narrative histories, for imagination supplies much that theory can but too imperfectly convey where it has no data. What is least usefully informative about music as an art is the section dealing with Oriental instruments, for although we can still hear the music of the East to-day very much as it must have been in ancient times, it is so completely divorced from our own as to be of no significance to our musical history. That is why after p. 29 the extra-European countries are dismissed for good and all. Nevertheless, they had to be included at this early stage, for a glance at these illustrations shows that the origin of every type of European instrument can be traced back to the East. The Occident supplied mechanical improvements — the keyboard is a notable one — but originated nothing.

To be a profitable source of information on the nature and the developments of the art of music these pictures should be studied in connexion with musico-historical literature; they will prove extraordinarily elucidating and help to impress facts upon the memory astonishingly. To books of reference, such as Grove's *Dictionary*, they are an invaluable supplement, even though that work is itself profusely illustrated. But if here they can merely follow such literary productions as Ambros's monumental *History* revised by Leichtentritt or the *Oxford History*, they definitely take the lead as a record of musical evolution considered as an aspect of human culture. No literary work on the subject can approach them as a demonstration of the indisputable fact that music is not an art which flourished in isolation, though Cecil Gray's recent *History* makes a brave attempt in this direction. That music would have been a vastly different thing but for its close alliance with the other arts, and that it influenced them in turn, has never been so convincingly shown as here.

It is in the nature of the case that what appears most clearly is its relation to the arts and crafts of sculpture, painting, drawing, engraving, and printing. Its indebtedness to the theatre is scarcely less evident and its close alliance to the dance is illustrated with particular charm. Even architecture, the art most remote from music in practice, though Schelling's definition of it as frozen music brings their aesthetic ideals into proximity, is represented by views of various European opera houses. It must be confessed that music's nearest associate, literature, takes no place adequate to its importance in this book, not only because the connexion is obvious at every step in the evolution of the brother and sister arts, but because the inclusion of relevant pictures would have gone very much too far. Because innumerable operas have been based on subjects from Shakespeare, Goethe, Walter Scott, and Victor Hugo, because poems by Burns, Heine, Verlaine, and a hundred others have been endlessly set to music, it would have been preposterous to give portraits of even the outstanding figures in literature who indirectly enriched music. Yet even here the book is not found altogether wanting. Literary lights like Quinault and Metastasio, who as librettists had a great deal to do with the progress of opera, are duly present, and a minor personage like the Rev. Thomas Morell, who is now remembered only as Handel's librettist, justifies his place in a work like this. As for writers on music, who in truth rarely shine as literary craftsmen, they are liberally represented.

Even more than its alliance with the other arts, music here shows its fusion with the whole cultural setting and atmosphere of any given period.   We see it taking a hand in the services of the church and the entertainments of the stage, follow it to the courts of princes and into the homes of the people, watch minstrels and town musicians engaged in its cult for their living, cloistered and chambered folk toying with it for love.   These pictures cannot let us hear the music, but they somehow give a more vivid impression of its feeling and flavour at any period of its history than the most brilliant verbal description could do.   Where the music is actually lost to us or no longer affords us aesthetic satisfaction, they are suggestive to a surprising degree, while that which we happily still possess and are still able to delight in seems to take on a new significance and colour and variety once we are familiar with its original environment. And, above all, pictures have this advantage over the written word: they tell the truth, neither more nor less — truth unwarped by sentimentality and unembroidered by too exuberant an imagination or enthusiasm.

ERIC BLOM

London, October 1929.

TABLE OF CONTENTS

1

3

5

2

4

Examples of Sumerian and Hittite art: (1) Drummer.   Fragment of a Sumerian steatite vessel, of the period of Gudea, the priest-king.   Latter half of the third millennium B.C.   Paris, Musée du Louvre.   (2) Sacrificial scene, with a harper. Relief on a limestone pillar from the Sumerian king's palace at Tello.   Gudea's period.   Paris, Louvre.   (3) Lute player (shepherd and dog).   Sumerian clay relief.   Middle or end of the third millennium B.C.   Philadelphia, Pennsylvania Museum. (4) and (5) Trumpeter and guitar player.   Panel from the wall surrounding the Hittite Royal Castle at Üjuk.   Beginning of the first millennium B.C.   Constantinople, Ottoman Museum.

1   2

3

(**1**) Lute player. Basalt panel from east side of outer fortress tower of Sendschirli. Ninth century B.C. Berlin, State Museum (collection of West-Asiatic antiquities). (**2**) Harper. Alabaster relief from the palace of the Assyrian king, Assurnasirpal (883–859 B.C.) in Nimrud. London, British Museum. (**3**) Musicians in procession. Drummers (tympanumists) and lute players. Basalt panel from the north wall of the hall of Sendschirli. Second half of the eighth century B.C. Constantinople, Ottoman Museum.

1

3

2   4

(1)–(3) Procession of musicians (harpers, lyre players, double-pipe players, and others).   Wall relief from the royal palace in Kuyundshik (ruins of Nineveh), eighth and seventh century B.C.   Time of King Sennacherib (705–681) and King Assurbanipal (668–626).   (1) and (2) London, British Museum.   (3) Paris, Musée du Louvre.   (4) Procession of musicians. Fragment of a Phoenician ivory box, from the palace at Nimrud.   c. ninth century B.C.   London, British Museum.

1

2

Period of the ancient kingdom, fourth to sixth dynasty: (1) Female harpists, hand-clappers, and flute players. Wall painting from the tomb of Snofrujenashtef in Daschour. Fourth dynasty. 2825 B.C. Period of King Snofru. Cairo, Museum of Egyptian Antiquities. (2) Musicians, hand-clappers, singers, and female dancers. Wall relief from the tomb of Nensheftkai in Saggara. Fifth dynasty. c. 2700 B.C. Also in the Cairo Museum.

1

3   2   4

New kingdom period (seventeenth to twentieth dynasty): (**1**) Lady eating a meal, musicians with harp, lute, and manual drum. Wall painting from the tomb of Rechmere in Schech abd el Gurna. Eighteenth dynasty. *c.* 1475 B.C. Time of King Thutmos III. (**2**) Musicians with double hautboy, lute, and harp. Wall painting from the tomb of Nacht in Thebes. Also of the time of Thutmos III. (**3**) and (**4**) Lyre and harp players. Wall painting from the tomb of Zeser-kereseneb in Schech abd el Gurna. Eighteenth dynasty. 1415 B.C. Time of Thutmos IV.

I

3   2   4

(1) Syrian Bedouins playing the lyre.   From a wall painting in Beni Hassan.   Twelfth dynasty, 1900 B.C. (middle kingdom period).   (2) Dancing girls with hoop drums and clappers at a funeral.   Limestone relief from a tomb in Saggara.   Late in the eighteenth dynasty, after 1400 B.C.   Cairo Museum.   (3) and (4) Triangular harp and 'tub' drum players, lyre, and lute player.   Limestone relief from the time of the Persian rule.   Fourth century B.C.   Alexandria Museum.

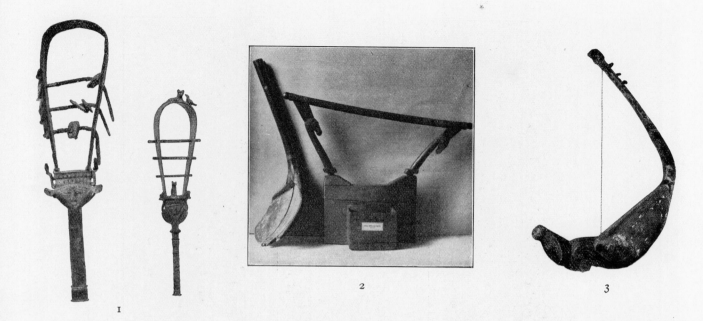

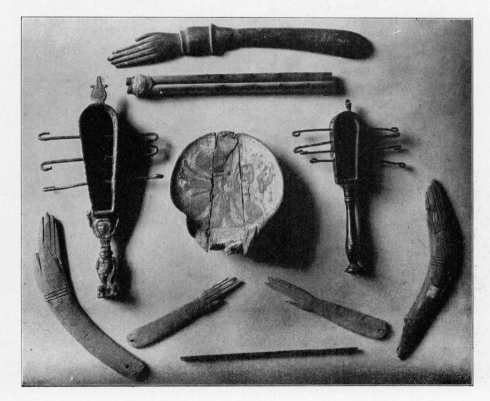

Egyptian instruments: (1) Two sistrums (temple rattles, Saissite) of bronze, twenty-second to twenty-fifth dynasty, about 1000–600 B.C. London, British Museum. (2) Stand harp (left) and lyre (right). Berlin, Egyptian Museum. (3) Painted stand harp. Eighteenth dynasty, 1450 B.C. London, British Museum. (4) Group of Egyptian instruments. Arm clappers (of ivory, bone, and wood). Double clarinet, bronze sistrum. Sounding board of a bow harp, reeds. Berlin, Egyptian Museum.

(1) and (2) Aulos blower (side and front view).   (3) and (4) Harpist (trigonon, triangular frame harp, side and front view).
Marble idols from Keros, in the island of Amorgos.   Cyclades art of the second half of the third millennium B.C.   Athens,
National Museum.

(1) and (2) Sacrificial procession with aulos and lyre player from a limestone sarcophagus found at Hagia Triada in Crete. 1300 B.C.   Heraclion Museum.   (3) Reapers' procession with singers and sistrum players.   Upper part of a Cretan steatite vessel.   1500 B.C.   Heraclion Museum.   (4) Processional dance with a lyre player.   Painting on the neck of a hydria from Analatos in Attica.   700 B.C.   Athens, National Museum.   (5) Cymbal players.   Oriental Greek thin disk of bronze with embossed reliefs from the Mount Ida Zeus grotto in Crete.   After 750 B.C.   Heraclion Museum.   (6) Cithara player. Fragment of an embossed bronze sheet from Olympia.   End of the eighth century B.C.

(1) Dirge of the Nereids over the corpse of Achilles, and a lyre carrier.   From a Corinthian hydria from Cervetri. 550 B.C.
Paris, Louvre.   Photograph by Alinari.   (2) Cithara player on pedestal.   From an amphora of the workshop of the potter
Andokides at Vulci.   530 B.C.   Paris, Louvre.   Photograph by Alinari.   (3) Aulos player stepping on to the pedestal.
From a cup of the vase-painter Euphronius.   510 B.C.   Paris, Louvre.   (4) Drinker playing double aulos; the case of
the instrument hangs in front of him.   Painting inside an Attic drinking bowl from Orvieto.   500 B.C.   Boston, Museum
of Fine Arts.   (5) Female dancer and player on the aulos, its case on the right.   On an Attic lecythos from Gela.   460 B.C.
Syracuse, National Museum.   (6) Acrobats with an aulos player and spectators.   On an Attic amphora from Kamiros
in Rhodes.   535 B.C.   Paris, Bibliothèque Nationale.

(1) Aulos player (with the mouth-band, called Phorbeia) and dancer with krotals at a symposium. From a drinking-dish by the potter Python and the vase-painter Epictetos. From Vulei. 510 B.C. London, British Museum. (2) Komast with lyre. From a drinking-dish by the vase-painter Skythes. 510 B.C. Rome, Villa Giulia. (3) Silenus with cithara. From an Attic cup. 460 B.C. Vienna, Art History Museum. (4) Women playing with harp (sambyke), cithara, and lyre. On a South Italian volute cup. End of the fifth century B.C. Munich, Vase Collection. (5) Girl tuning a cithara. Brightly-coloured drinking-dish. 470 B.C. Paris, Louvre.

(1) Orpheus playing the lyre among the Thracians. On an Attic cup from Gela. 440 B.C. Berlin, Vase Collection.
(2) Komasts with lyre and aulos. Drinking-dish from the workshop of Brygos. 480 B.C. Wurzburg, University Art History Museum. (3) Aulos player at the preparations for a symposium. Resonating vessel from Cervetri. 540 B.C. Boston, Museum of Fine Arts. (4) Lesson in lyre playing (Iphitos and Linos). Cithara above, in centre. Drinking-vessel (Skyphos) from the workshop of Pistoxenos. 475 B.C. Schwerin, State Museum. (5) and (6) Komasts with vine stalk, cithara, and krotals, victorious cithara player on a pedestal, from an Attic amphora of about 480 to 430 B.C. Rome, Vatican (Museo Gregoriano). Photograph by Alinari.

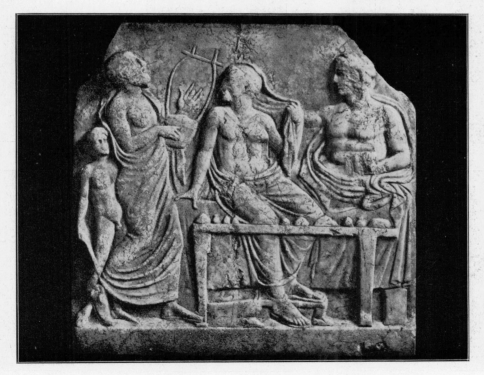

(1) Lyre player.   Side panel of an altar (?) in Parian marble.   465 B.C.   Boston, Museum of Fine Arts.   (2) Girl playing the aulos. Similar side panel. Rome, Museo Nazionale. (3) Singer with lyre at a symposium. Marble relief, Greek mainland art.   End of the fifth century B.C.   Rome, Museo Barracco.   Photograph by Alinari.

(**1**) Three Muses. Left: aulos; right: lute. Marble relief from Mantinea. Work of the younger Praxiteles. 300 B.C. Athens, National Museum. (**2**) Satyr with foot-clapper (krupezion). Restored Roman copy of a Greek marble statue. Florence, Uffizi. (**3**) Lute player. Terra-cotta figure from Tanagra. Paris, Louvre. Photograph by Alinari. (**4**) Satyr with syrinx. Bronze statuette from Pergamon. Berlin, Antiquarium. (**5**) Lute-playing Eros. Late Hellenistic terra-cotta figure from Kom-es-Shufaka in Egypt. Stuttgart Museum. (**6**) Tomb stele of Niko with cithara. Limestone sculpture from Alexandria. Cairo Museum. (**7**) Eros blowing German flute. Terra-cotta figure from Megara. Paris, Louvre. All these are of the third to second century B.C.

(**1**) Two bronze (German) flutes (plagiauloi) with busts of Maenads on the mouthpiece. London, British Museum. (**2**) Pair of bronze basins (cymbals).   London, British Museum.   (**3**) and (**4**) Sounding box of a bronze lyre with figures in relief. From Pantikapaion, the modern Kertsch, Crimea.

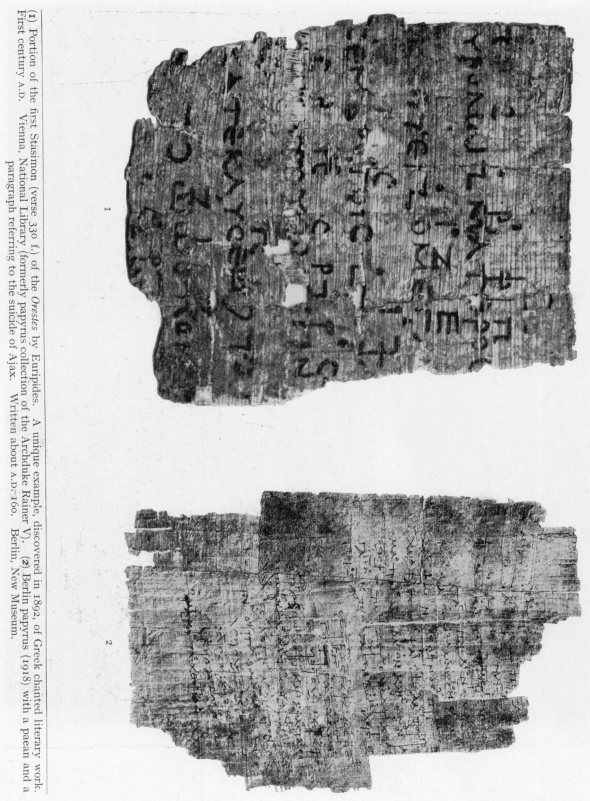

1

2

(1) Portion of the first Stasimon (verse 330 f.) of the *Orestes* by Euripides. A unique example, discovered in 1892, of Greek chanted literary work. First century A.D. Vienna, National Library (formerly papyrus collection of the Archduke Rainer V). (2) Berlin papyrus (1918) with a paean and a paragraph referring to the suicide of Ajax. Written about A.D. 160. Berlin, New Museum.

1

2

3

4

(**1**) Youth playing the aulos.   Restored wall painting by an Hellenistic painter from the Vigna Ammendola on the Appian Way near Rome.   London, British Museum.   (**2**) Cithara player.   Wall painting (in the so-called second Pompeian style) from a villa near Boscoreale.   Supposed copy of a painting of the first half of the third century B.C.   New York, Metropolitan Museum. (**3**) Harp player.   Wall painting from the summer-house of the Farnesina at Rome.   End of first century B.C.   Rome, Museo Nazionale.   (**4**) Lyre player.   Pompeian wall painting, a supposed copy of a painting of the third century B.C.   Naples, Museo Nazionale.

1

2

3

4

(**1**) Sistrum player. Marble sarcophagus of a priestess of Isis and her husband. About A.D. 50. Athens, National Museum. (**2**) Lute players. Part of Roman marble sarcophagus. Second century A.D. Paris, Louvre. (**3**) Priest of Cybele (Archigallus) with various instruments. First half of the second century A.D. Rome, Conservatory Palace. (**4**) Sacrificial scene with musical accompaniment (tuba and double tibia). Marble relief from a monument to the Emperor Marcus Aurelius in Ephesus. A.D. 165. Vienna, Art History Museum.

I

2

3

(**1**) Dionysus procession.   Maenads playing cymbals and aulos with movable rings, from which later the stops were evolved. Marble relief of A.D. 50.   Naples, Museo Nazionale.   Photograph by Brogi.   (**2**) Silenus (with the so-called Phrygian flute) and Maenads.   On a marble sarcophagus from Patras.   Before A.D. 150.   Athens, National Museum.   Photograph by Alinari. (**3**) Funeral games with actors and a cithara player.   Marble relief from a sarcophagus.   A.D. 250.   Rome, Villa Doria-Pamfili. Photograph by Bruckmann.

(1) Gladiatorial combat accompanied by musical instruments.   Tuba, organ, two horns (buccina or cornua). Mosaic pavement of a Roman villa near Zliten in Tripoli. Third century A.D. (2) Hornblowers (buccinatores or cornicines) of the Roman army.   Limestone relief from the round temple dedicated in A.D. 109 by the Emperor Trajan to Mars Ultor at Adamklissa in the Dobrudscha. Bucharest Museum.   (3) Tombstone of the Roman cavalry trumpeter Andes. Limestone relief, second half of the first century A.D.   Mayence, collection of the Society of Antiquarians.   (4) Tuba players and gladiators. Part of a marble relief. A.D. 50.   Munich, Glyptothek. (5) Trumpets from the Temple of Jerusalem. Relief on the Arch of Titus, dedicated at Rome in A.D. 81.

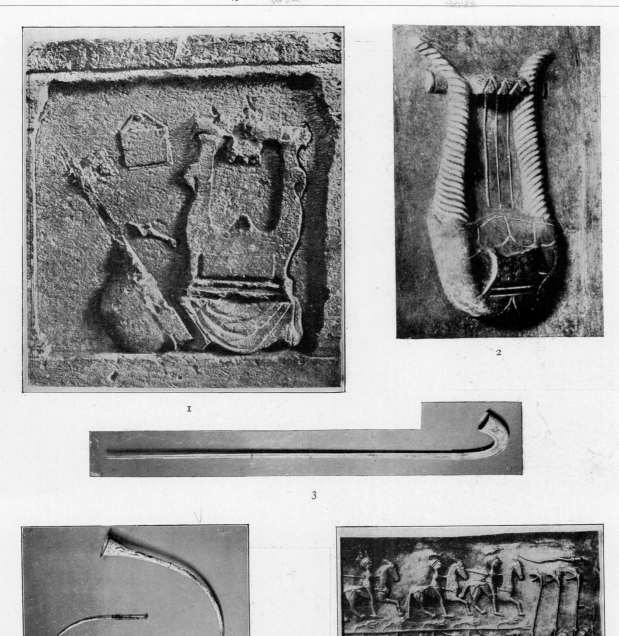

(1) Lute and cithara, between them a book of notes and a plectrum.   Relief from the limestone sarcophagus of a Roman musician.   Second to third century A.D.   Arles Museum.   (2) Lyre with frame made of antelope horns.   Relief from the tomb of the poetess Petronia Musa.   Before A.D. 150.   Rome, Villa Borghese.   (3) Lituus (Roman trumpet).   Facsimile of an instrument (found 1827 in Cervetri) in the Vatican Museum at Rome.   Leipzig, Heyer Collection.   (4) Buccina (tuba curva, cornu: Roman war horn).   Facsimile of an instrument dug up in Pompeii, now in the Vatican Museum at Rome.   Leipzig, Heyer Collection.   (5) Band of Celtic warriors with trumpets.   Relief inside a silver vessel from Gundestrup, Jutland.   First century B.C. to first century A.D.   Copenhagen, National Museum.

1

2

3

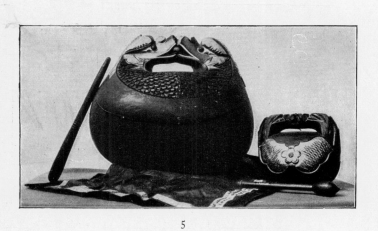

4

5

(1) Yün lo, set of Chinese temple and palace gongs.   (2) Wooden figure of a Buddhist monk (Taoist) playing on a Mu yü (wooden fish, see No. 5).   (3) Taiko, Japanese large drum with painted skins, in a wooden stand.   (4) Tsuzumi and kakko, small Japanese drums.   (5) Ao yü and Mu yü, drums of fish shape.   Used by Chinese priests.   All these are in the Ethnological Museum at Leipzig.

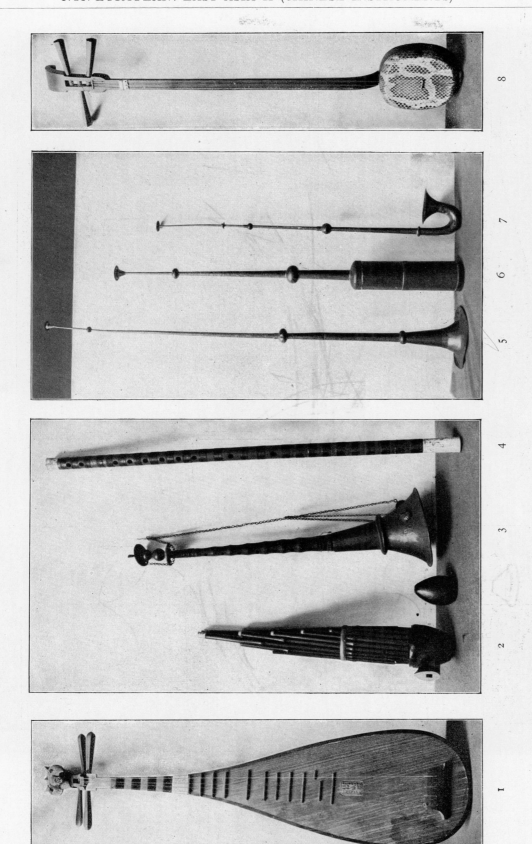

(1) P'i p'a (Japanese: Biwa), four-stringed Chinese lute with bat's head. (2) Seng (Japanese: So), Chinese wind instrument with vibrating reeds (mouth-organ, precursor of the European harmonium). (3) Heang teih or So na (Japanese: Carumera), Chinese pipes (corresponding to the Persian Zurna and the Indian Sanai) with brass ornaments and sounding piece. (4) Ti tzo, Chinese (so-called German) flute of bamboo stem. (5)–(7) La pa, Hao t'ung (Huang teih, Japanese: Dokaku), Ca Kiao (Tung keo), Chinese trumpets, which are also used for ritual purposes at funerals and weddings. (8) Samisen (=three-stringed), East Asiatic long-necked plucked-string instrument with snake-skin cover. All these are in the Ethnological Museum, Leipzig.

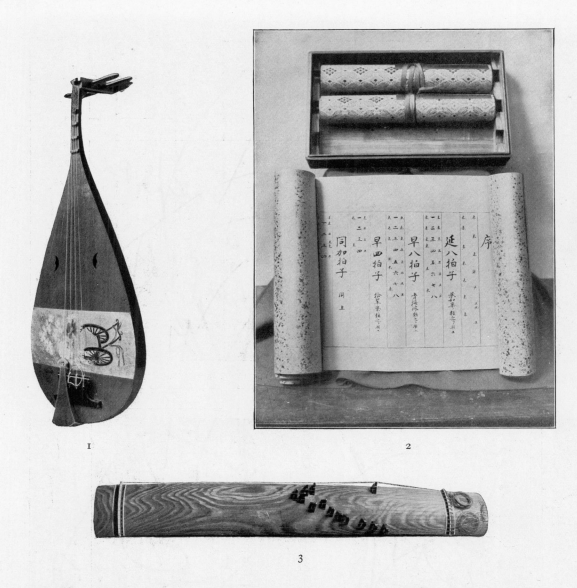

(1) Biwa, four-stringed Japanese lute (like the Chinese p'i p'a) with its 'batsi' or plectrum.   (2) Three rolls of Japanese music in wooden box.   (3) Sonokoto (takikoto), a large thirteen-stringed Japanese koto, the favourite instrument of Japanese ladies.   (4) Yang k'in ('foreign string player'), fourteen-stringed Chinese dulcimer, santer, introduced from West Asia (Arabia and Persia).   All these are in the Ethnological Museum, Leipzig.

1

2

3

4

(1) and (2) Women playing the samisen.   (3) Women playing the koto.   Woodcut by Suzuki Harunobu (about 1725–70).
(4) Female flute players (Gensoo and Yokihi).   Woodcut by Kitagawa Utamaro (1753–1806).

(**1**) Kemânge, Persian four-stringed bow instrument, with its bow (kemân).   (**2**) King of Heaven (ruler of the east side of Mount Meru) playing on the small lute (Chinese p'i p'a; Thibetan pi-wang).   Thibetan gilt wooden figure, coated with gypsum.   (**3**) Tanbur, Persian-Arabic long-necked, four-stringed lute.   (**4**) Two damaru (Thibetan, cang teu), Thibetan double drums with human brain-pans for resonating parts.   All in the Ethnological Museum, Leipzig.

(**1**) and (**2**) Sârindâ (front and side view), Bengal three-stringed bow instrument, derived from the sârangî. Leipzig, Ethnological Museum. (**3**) A Burmese playing the bow harp (Burmese: tsaun) (see No. 3, p. 7). Model in wax made for the Frankfort Music Exhibition, 1927. Photograph by Dr. P. Wolff, Frankfort-on-Main. (**4**) Pattala (Siamese: ranat), Burmese wooden slab instrument (xylophone), with twenty-two tuned bamboo strips, the chief instrument in Burma. Leipzig, Ethnological Museum.

3

4

5

(1) Muralî (Bengal), flute of bamboo stem, found in Delhi and Sumatra.   (2) Tiktiri (Sanskrit), North Indian double clarinet, with gourd reservoir; the 'charm' instrument of the snake-charmers throughout Lower India. (3) Burmese orchestras, each with a great gong and drum (Burmese: kye-vain, tshain-vain) in the foreground.   (1 to 3, Ethnological Museum, Leipzig.) (4) Tamburi (tumburu-vina), large Lower Indian lute with four wire strings. Leipzig, Heyer Collection. (5) Java-nese orchestra ('Gamelan').   Hamburg, Ethnological Museum.   Photograph by Dr. P. Wolff, Frankfort-on-Main.

(1) Drum of the Bule negroes (South Cameroons).   (2) Beaked flutes with note holes (pitos) from Mexico.   London, British Museum.   (3) Marimba (balafo), East African instrument with seventeen scaled plates of wood, and gourds for resonance. Leipzig, Heyer Collection.   (4) Carved figure of a negress carrying a drum.   (5) Two kissars, North African lyres in the shape of the ancient five-stringed lyre of the god Hermes.   (1, 4, and 5, photographs by Dr. P. Wolff from exhibits in the Frankfort Music Exhibition, 1927.)

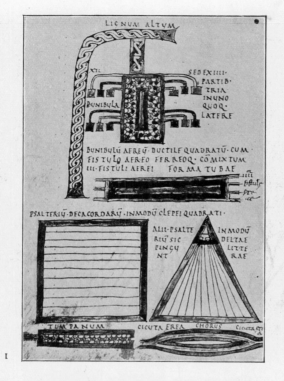

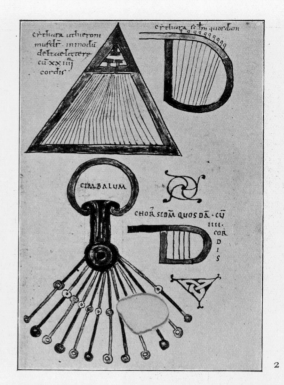

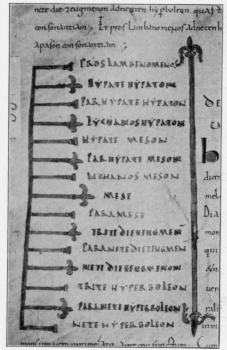

(1) and (2) Ancient illustrations of instruments in a treatise *De Musica* composed by the Roman Anicius Manlius Severinus Boethius (*c.* 475–524). As it is the latest theoretical work of ancient times, it is the chief source of medieval musical science. Cod. Lat. 14523 of the State Library, Munich. (3) Representation of the Greek tonic system from Boethius' *De Musica*. Vienna, Collected Codex 55 in the National Library. (4) Representation of the medieval tonic system (in so-called Dasia Notation) from the *Musica Enchiriadis* of the monk Hucbald of St. Amand (840–930), a standard work for the study of the beginnings of music for several voices (organum). Vienna, Codex 55 of the National Library.

1   2   3

4

(1) King David playing the rotta, surrounded by musicians. Miniature from a codex of the eighth century. London, British Museum. (2) Rotta, the ancient North European cithara, from an early medieval Germanic warrior's grave, discovered in 1846 near Oberflacht in the Württemberg Black Forest. Berlin, Ethnological Museum. (3) Notker Balbulus, a monk at St. Gallen (830–912), one of the oldest and most important composers of sequences. Likeness by a contemporary monk of St. Gallen (from the Proceedings of the Antiquarian Society, Zurich, vol. xix, part 4). (4) Sequences of the eleventh century with St. Gallen 'Neumes' set alongside (see p. 33). Salzburg Gradual (Christmas Office) of 1060, St. Peter's Writing School. Vienna, Codex 1845 of the National Library.

Representations of instruments from the Utrecht Psalter, a Carolingian illustrated manuscript of the ninth century (860), which is of great importance for the study of the musical instruments of the Middle Ages. (1) Group of musicians, in the foreground an organ with two organists and four blowers. (2) Harp and fiddle with long bow (the fidula mentioned in Otfried's *Harmony of the Gospel*). (3) Rotta (lyre and small harp). (4) Organ. (5) Long-necked lute (similar to the Asiatic 'tanbur'). Utrecht, University Library.

The medieval Neume system, evolved from pre-Christian ceremonial song, showed the general course of the melody, without giving the rise and fall of the notes; it merely served to aid the memory of the singer. (1) and (2) Sheet 36 v. and 37 r. of the autograph Tonarium (compilations of Gregorian church chants). *De Harmonica Institutione* of the Benedictine Abbot Regino von Prüm (died 915). Leipzig, City Historical Museum. (3) Hymn: *Laudi omnipotens ferimus*. From the Collected Codex 843 of the National Library, Vienna.

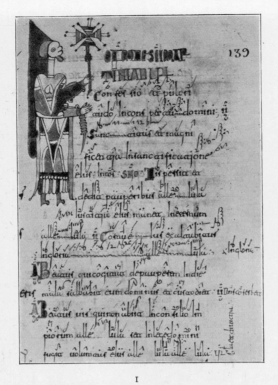

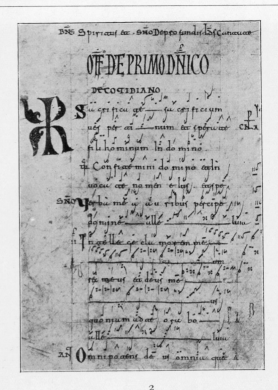

1

2

3

4

(1) and (2) Codices with Mozarabic (West Gothic) Neumes of the tenth and eleventh centuries. (Mozarabs are the Christian Arabs in Spain on whom Pope Gregory VII forced the Roman liturgy.) London, British Museum: Add. MSS. 30845 and 30851. (3) Troparium of the tenth century. Vienna, Collected Codex 1609 of the National Library. (4) Antiphonary of the twelfth century. Einsiedeln (Switzerland), Monastery Library.

(1) Rotta player, one of the capitals representing the eight 'finals' of the ecclesiastical modes in the choir of the old monastery church at Cluny. Early twelfth century. Cluny Museum. (2) Jug (so-called aquamanile) with two musicians (timbrel and early transverse flute). From an excavation in Upper Hungary. Eleventh to twelfth centuries. Budapest, National Museum. Photograph by Stoedtner. (3) to (6) Musicians with various instruments: centre of fig. 6 shows performers manipulating a hurdy-gurdy (organistrum). Carvings from the archbishop's palace at Santiago de Compostela, ancient capital of the kingdom of Galicia (Corunna, Spain). End of the twelfth century.

(1) Angel with bombard.   (2) Ménétrier (minstrel) with gittern: figures from Rheims Cathedral.   Middle or first half of
thirteenth century.   (3) Angel playing rebec; from the choir of Cologne Cathedral.   First half of the fourteenth century.
(4) Angel with hurdy-gurdy (organistrum, symphonia).   Florentine marble figure.   End of fourteenth century.   Vienna,
Liechtenstein Gallery.   Photograph by Wolfrum.   (5) Orpheus as lute player.   Relief by Giotto (or Andrea Pisano)
from the Campanile, Florence.   First half of the fourteenth century (about 1340).   Photograph by Brogi.

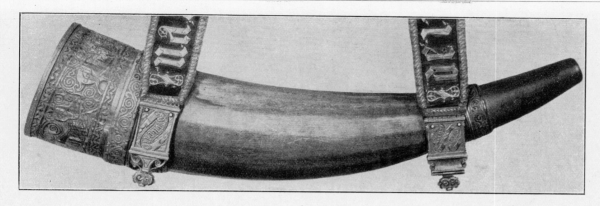

I

2

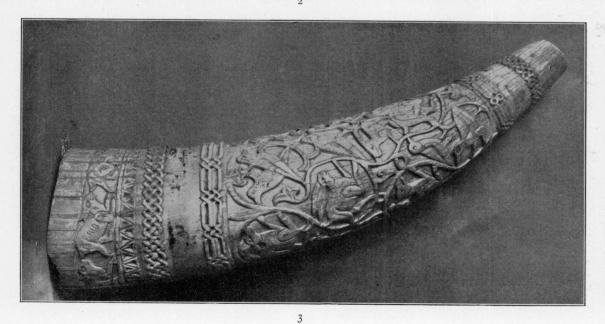

3

The oliphant, a carved hunting-horn made from an elephant's tusk, was brought to the West from Byzantium in the tenth and eleventh centuries and, with the sword, was among the most valuable items of a knight's equipment. (1) The so-called Horn of Charlemagne, said to be a gift from Haroun al Raschid, but actually an eleventh-century product. Aix-la-Chapelle, cathedral treasury. (2) Richly carved oliphant with later—probably spurious—inscription, stating that the horn was bestowed upon the monastery of Muri in the Aargau by the Habsburg landgrave Albert III in 1199. Western workmanship of the twelfth century (?). Vienna, Art History Museum. (3) Richly carved oliphant of Eastern origin. From the Ambraser Kunstkammer. Vienna, Art History Museum.

(1) Musicians blowing oliphants and plucking fiddle (cf. No. 3, p. 39).   (2) Dancers with fiddle and bow.   From the *Beati Commentarius*, Add. MSS. 11695.   London, British Museum.   (3) Christ surrounded by the twenty-four apocalyptic elders (with various instruments: organ, psaltery, oliphant, fiddle, harp, etc.).   Add. MSS. 17333.   London, British Museum. Photograph by the Art Historical Institute, Marburg. (4) King David as harpist between four musicians, playing glocken-spiel (bells), fiddle, zinke (or cornet), and organ.   From an illustrated Bible, Pommersfelden, Schönborn Library. Photograph by Dr. P. Wolff, Frankfort. (5) Similar group, the musicians having cornets, harp, panpipes, and fiddle. MS. Lat. 11550.   Paris, Bibliothèque Nationale.

(1) to (5) King David playing harp, organistrum, rebec, and psaltery. From the Psalter Cod. Lat. 3900. Munich, Staatsbibliothek. (6) King David playing rotta, surrounded by musicians with rebec, glockenspiel, long horn (Heerhorn), and
organ. From the so-called prayer-book of St. Elizabeth. Vienna, National Library. (7) King David as organist and
Pope Gregory I, founder of the Gregorian chant (reigned 590–604), with monochord. From Cod. Lat. 17403 (1241).
Munich, Staatsbibliothek.

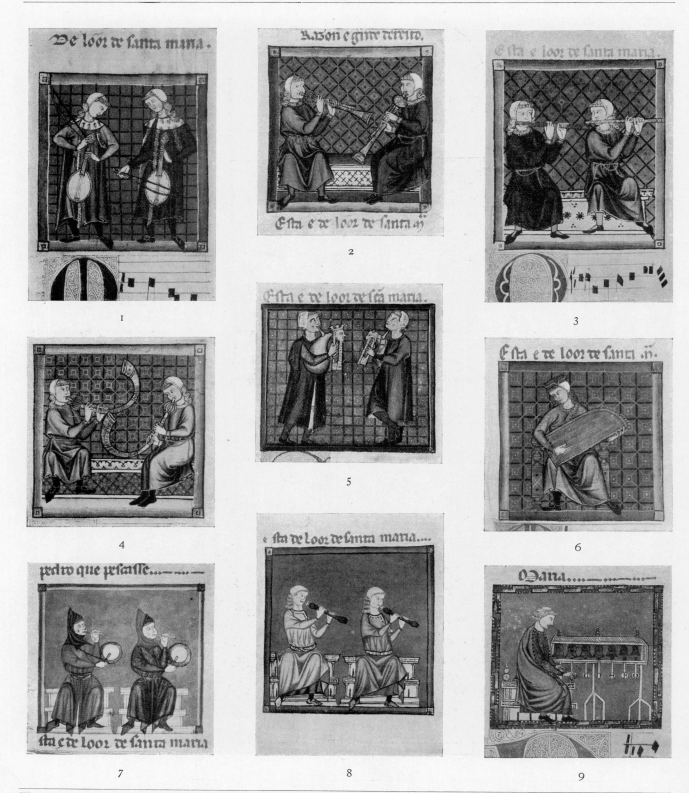

The miniatures of the third codex of the *Cantigas de Santa Maria*, by Alfonso el Sabio (Alfonso X), King of Leon and Castile from 1254 to 1284, and preserved in the Escurial Library, are among the most important pictorial records of medieval instruments.   (**1**) Fiddles (vihuelas de arco, viole da gamba); (**2**) double platerspiel (doppioni?) (=rudimentary bagpipe); (**3**) transverse flutes (axabebas); (**4**) curved platerspiel (=rudimentary bagpipe); (**5**) bagpipes; (**6**) psaltery; (**7**) one-hand flutes (galoubets) with drums (=pipes and tabors); (**8**) shawms; (**9**) glockenspiel (bells).

1

2

3

4

The so-called Manasse manuscript—preserved in the University Library at Heidelberg and more appropriately named: *The Great Heidelberg Song-script* (Große Heidelberger Liederhandschrift)—is by far the most precious of all extant Middle High-German minnesinger manuscripts.   It was written in the beginning of the fourteenth century in Switzerland, and contains 137 full-page miniatures.   (1) Psaltery; (2) 'her Reinmar der Vidiller' with fiddle; (3) harp; (4) group of musicians (under the portrait of Meister Heinrich Frauenlob) with fiddles, shawm, flute with drum (=pipe and tabor), and bagpipe.

1

2

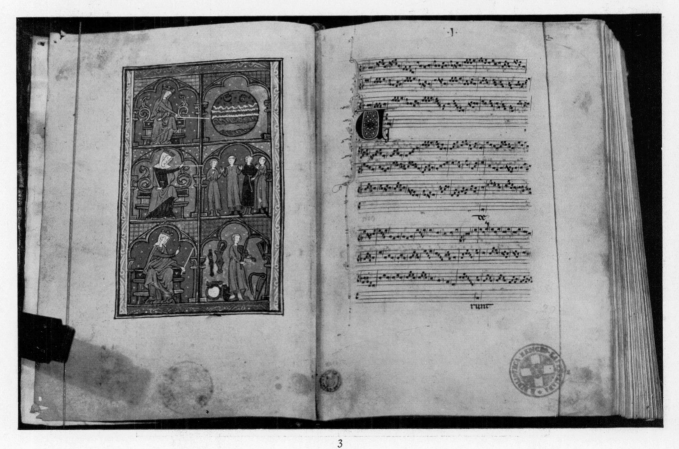

3

(1) Hymnal with neumes and lines (red line F, yellow line middle C). First half of the fourteenth century (1366). MS. 1000, library of the Klosterneuburg Stift. (2) English six-part canon (rota): *Sumer is icumen in* (*c.* 1240), written down by John of Fornsete, a monk of Reading Abbey; the oldest known canon and one of the first examples of 'measured' (mensural) music. The notation is the so-called 'Nota quadrata' of the Roman chorals. Harleian MS. 978 f. 11 v. London, British Museum. (3) Antiphonarium Mediceum (*Liber Petri de Medicis Cos[imi] Fil[ii]*) in early mensural notation with ligatures. Thirteenth century. Florence, Biblioteca Laurenziana. Photograph by Dr. P. Wolff, Frankfort.

(1) Gravestone of the blind composer Francesco Landino (c. 1325–97), the greatest of the Florentine *ars nova* group in the fourteenth century. Florence, Basilica San Lorenzo. Photograph by Alinari. (2) Antiphonary in Roman choral-notation of the fourteenth century which was still not far removed from the Neumatic. Add. MSS. 12; 194. London, British Museum. (3) The Arundel Psalter in Roman choral-notation (final phase). MS. Ar. 83. London, British Museum.

(**1**) School of Giotto (Taddeo Gaddi): angels playing (cornets, psaltery, rebec), section of the 'Coronation of the Virgin' (*c.* 1335). Florence, S. Croce. (**2**) Simoni Martini (master of the Siennese School): from the 'Legend of St. Martin' (double flute, mandora) (*c.* 1330). Assisi, S. Francesco. (**3**) Antonio Veneziano? (certainly not Taddeo Gaddi): from the 'Triumph of the Church' (portative organ) (*c.* 1360–70). Florence, Cappella della Spagnioli in S. Maria Novella. (**4**) School of Giotto (not Orcagna): from the 'Triumph of Death' (psaltery, rebec). Pisa, Camposanto. Photographs by Alinari and Anderson.

I

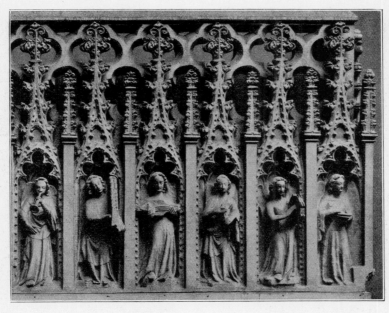

2

The minstrel gallery in the north triforium of the nave of Exeter Cathedral (built 1230–1370) is one of the most exquisite monuments in the northern sculpture of the late Middle Ages. The twelve angels, set up in niches, are playing the following instruments: lute, bagpipe, shawm, rebec, harp, jew's harp, trumpet or clarion, portative organ, gittern, flute-à-bec, timbrel, and cymbals. Photograph by the Victoria and Albert Museum, London.

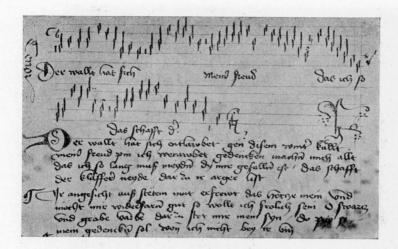

(**1**) *Der Wald hat sich entlaubet* from the Lochheimer Song-book, produced in or near Nuremberg (1455–60), an invaluable source for old German folk-song in parts. Wernigerode, Fürstliche Stollbergsche Bibliothek. (Reproduction by the Wölbing-Verlag, Berlin.) (**2**) *Ain Graserin durch kuehlen Tau* from Oswald von Wolkenstein's Song-book (see portrait, fig. 4), written in 1425. German choral-notation. MS. 2777. Vienna, Nationalbibliothek. (**3**) *Tagelied* from the so-called Mondseer MS. (also called Spörl's Song-book) of the monk Hermann, who was attached to the Salzburg court (1365–96). German choral notation. MS. 2856 (fourteenth to fifteenth centuries). Vienna, Nationalbibliothek. (**4**) Oswald von Wolkenstein (1377–1445), one of the last of the minnesingers. Contemporary portrait miniature from the song-manuscript of the University Library, Innsbruck.

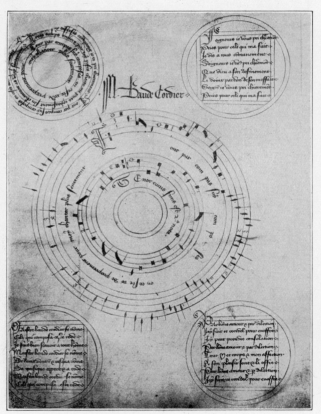

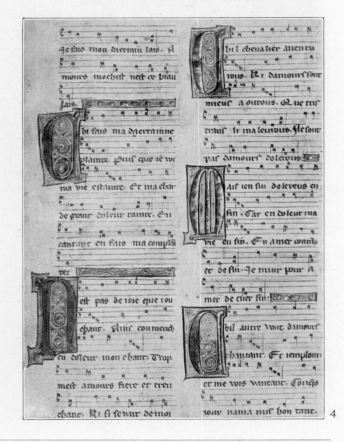

(**1**) Puzzle-canon by Baude Cordier, one of the first writers of the French art-song (rondeau) introduced by the Florentine *ars nova* (fourteenth century). Mensural notation of the fifteenth century. Cod. 1047. Chantilly, Bibliothèque et musée Condé. (**2**) From the *Estoires de Tristan, qu'on apele le bret* (troubadour songs). Roman choral-notation. MS. 2542, year 1477. Vienna, Nationalbibliothek. (**3**) Jean Fouquet: Etienne Chevalier with St. Stephen and angels playing (flutes à bec, psaltery, guitar-fiddle, lute). From the *Etienne Chevalier Book of Hours* (*c.* 1470). Chantilly, Condé Museum. (**4**) The authors of the Psalter of Duke René II of Lorraine (reigned 1473–1508). MS. 601. Paris, Bibliothèque de l'Arsénal.

(**1**) Guillaume Dufay (*c.* 1400–74) and Giles Binchois (*c.* 1400–60), the two leading Flemish masters of the fifteenth century, both from the choir school of Cambrai.   Contemporary miniature from *Le Champion des dames* by Martin le Franc.   Paris, Bibliothèque nationale.   (**2**) A river party in May.   Bruges miniature, end of the sixteenth century.   London, British Museum.   (**3**) Group of musicians, including two trumscheit (marine trumpet) players.   Miniature from a Flemish illustrated Bible of 1435.   London, British Museum.   (**4**) Three-part mass: *Virgo parens Christi* by Jacques Barbireau (d. 1491), from the Wedding Codex composed for the Emperor Charles V in 1526.   Mensural notation.   MS. 1783.   Vienna, Nationalbibliothek.   (**5**) Codex of Flemish masses celebrating Emperor Maximilian I's marriage to Bianca Maria of Milan (November 1493).   MS. 5248.   Vienna, Art History Museum.

(1) Josquin des Prés (c. 1450–1521), greatest Netherland master of the turn of the fifteenth to sixteenth centuries.   Wood-cut after the portrait formerly in St. Gudule, Brussels.   (2) Group of musicians (oliphant, one-hand flute with drum [pipe and tabor], trumpet) from the engraving, 'The Feast of Herodias' by Israel van Meckenem (d. 1509).   (3) 'The Couple at the Fountain' (lute, harp).   Engraving by the same master.   (4) *Missa de Venerabili Sacramento* by Josquin des Prés.   Hymn-book in mensural notation of the sixteenth century.   Codex originally owned by the Fugger family.   MS. 4809.   Vienna, National Library.   (See also fig. 1, p. 72.)

1   2

Hubert and Jan van Eyck: Angels singing and playing (positive organ, harp, angular fiddle).   Side panels of the Ghent
altar-piece, 'The Adoration of the Lamb' (painted 1420, erected 1431).   Ghent, St. Bavon (until 1920: Berlin, Kaiser
Friedrich Museum).   Photographs by Hanfstaengl.

(1) Angels playing (lute, guitar-fiddle, small drum, cymbals, harp, discant viol). Carved frame to Martin Schöngauer's painting: 'Maria im Rosenhag' ('Mary in the Rose Bower'), 1473. St. Martin's Church, Kolmar. (2) Master of St. Severin: The hermit and two musicians (trumpet, zinken [cornet] or bombards) before the table of St. Severin. From the 'History of St. Severin.' About 1500 or shortly after. Cologne, Wallraf-Richartz Museum. Photograph by the Kunstgewerbe Museum, Cologne.

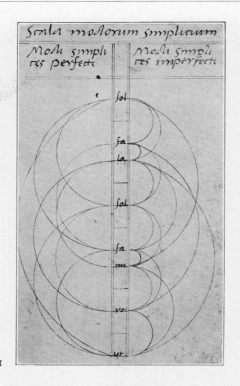

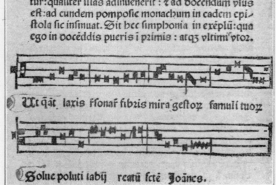

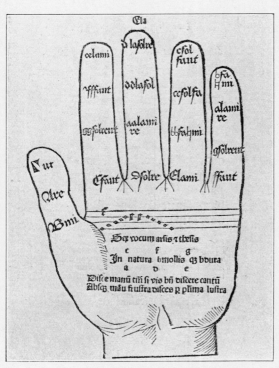

(1) From the (? spurious) treatise, *Musica Theorica*, by the Spaniard Bartolomeo Ramos de Pareja (*c.* 1440–*c.* 1500).   Mus. MS. Theor. 1310.   Berlin, Staatsbibliothek.   (2) From the *Treatise upon the Gamme* by the English musician Lionel Power (*c.* 1450, contemporary with Dunstable). Lansd. MS. 763. London, British Museum.   (3) From the *Musices Opusculum* by Nic. Burtius of Parma (1450–1518), published at Bologna in 1487; one of the oldest examples of printed mensural notation.   (4) The so-called 'Guidonic Hand' (Manus Guidonica), an aid to memory in learning the solmization system, introduced by Guido d'Arezzo, in which notes of the scale were indicated by syllables (see fig. 4, p. 37) instead of letters. From the *Flores musicae omnis cantus Gregoriani*, by Hugo Spechtshart von Reutlingen (1285/6–1359/60), published at Strasburg in 1488.

(1) Jean Charlier de Gerson, *Collectorium super Magnificat.* Esslingen, 1473, Conrad Fyner. First known attempt at music-printing; the notes are stamped on with dies. (2) *Missale Herbipolense* (Würzburg Missal). Würzburg, 1481, Jörg Ryser. One of the first missals with printed music (Typen-Doppeldruck). (3) *Lux bella*, Seville, 1492. The first Spanish printed music. (The printer's note reads: 'This work was printed in Seville by four German craftsmen in the year of Our Lord 1492.')

1

2

3

4

(1) Amusements at the Sign of the Planet Venus (one-hand flute with drum [pipe and tabor], hurdy-gurdy, platerspiel [rudimentary bagpipe], trumpets, zinke [cornet]). (2) Buffoons and travelling players ('fool's flute,' shawms, trumpet, lute, pipe, and tabor). Drawings from the so-called *Medieval House-book*, which appeared about 1475. Library of Schloss Wolfegg. (3) Organ player (at positive organ) and his wife. (4) 'The Lovers' (harp, lute, and lute-case). Engravings by Israel van Meckenem (cf. p. 55).

1

2

3

(**1**) The poetess Sappho (lute, harp, shawm, and mandora). Woodcut from Boccaccio's *Book of Famous Women*, Ulm, 1473. (**2**) 'The Masked Dancers' (one-hand flute and drum). Engraving by Israel van Meckenem. (**3**) Dance festival in Munich Castle. (In the galleries, musicians with transverse flute, drum, kettle-drums, and trumpets.) Engraving by the monogrammist M Z (? the goldsmith Matthäus Zasinger). Munich (*c.* 1500).

1

2

3

(**1**) Angels playing (guitar - fiddle, lute, clavichord). Portion of an 'Adoration of the Child.' Wood - carving, Northern Netherlands (*c.* 1450). Amsterdam, Rijksmuseum. Museum photograph. (**2**) Angels playing (portative, lute). Wood-carving. Organ loft, Strasburg Cathedral. Photograph by the Staatliche Bildstelle, Berlin. (**3**) Angels playing (shawm or discant - bombard, lute). Socle of a figure of the altar of Kefermarkt Church in Upper Austria, executed by Passau sculptors about 1480. Photograph by Reiffenberg.

(**1**) The organist Paul Hofhaimer (1459–1537) at a positive organ.   Woodcut by Hans Burgkmair from the 'Triumphzug' (Triumphal Procession) of the Emperor Maximilian I (see p. 76).   (**2**) Emperor Maximilian attending mass at Augsburg; in the left foreground: Hofhaimer at a so-called 'apple-regal.'   Woodcut by Hans Weiditz (*c.* 1518).   (**3**) 'Der Weisskunig beim Mummenschanz.'   (**4**) 'Die Geschicklichkeit in der Musik.'   Woodcuts by Hans Burgkmair from the prose novel *Der Weisskunig*, written in praise of the emperor (*c.* 1516).

The drawings for the celebrated woodcuts in *Kayser Maximilians I Triumph* were provided by Jörg Kölderer and his apprentices between 1507 and 1511. From 1516 onwards Hans Burgkmair was assisted in the execution of these masterly woodcuts by a number of other Augsburg and Nuremberg artists—Springinklee, Beck, Schäufelein, Dürer, and the so-called Meister des Trosses. (1) 'Musica Lauten vnd Rybeben' (viole da gamba). (2) 'Burgundische Pfeiffer' (trombones and bombards). (3) 'Musica Canterey' with singers, a trombonist and a Zinke (cornet) player. (4) 'Musica suess Melodey': rybebe (viola da gamba), harp, fiedel (viola da braccio), lutes, shawms (Windkapselschalmeien), Schwegel mit Tämerlin (pipe and tabor).

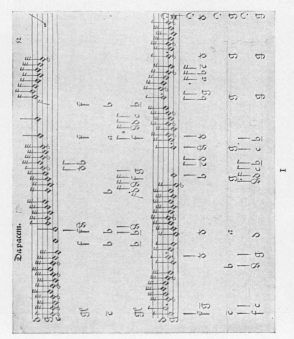

(1) From the *Tablaturen etlicher Lobgesang und Liedlein auf die Orgeln* by Arnold Schlick (see p. 74). *Getruckt zu Mentz* [Mainz] *durch Peter Schöffern . . . Anno MDXIII.'* (2) to (4) Organ tablature book of Elias Nicolaus Ammerbach (c. 1530–97), organist of the Thomaskirche, Leipzig, from 1560), Leipzig, 1571. Copy in the Leipzig Stadtbibliothek, formerly in the possession of Sebastian Bach. (2) Title-page. (3) Title-woodcut representing a singing-school. (4) Song: *Innsbruck, ich muß dich lassen* by Heinrich Isaac, arranged for German organ tablature, a combination of mensural and lettered notation in use with German organists until the eighteenth century.

1

2

3

4   5

(1) and (2) *Geistliches Gesangbüchlein*, compiled by Luther's friend and adviser Johann Walther (1496–1570), Kapell-meister to the court of Saxony.   Title-page to the tenor part-book and the choral, *Aus tiefer Not schrei' ich zu dir*, Mainz, 1525, Peter Schöffer the Younger.   (3) From *Etlich christlich Lobgesang*, the oldest Lutheran hymn-book, Wit-tenberg, 1523, Georg Rhau.   (4) Portrait of the reformer Martin Luther (1483–1525).   Woodcut by Lucas Cranach. (5) Title-page of the *Practica Musica* by the Wittenberg organist Hermann Finck (1527–58) with picture of a chantry (singers accompanied by a trumpeter and two krummhorn [cromorne] players).   Wittenberg, 1566, Georg Rhaus Erben.

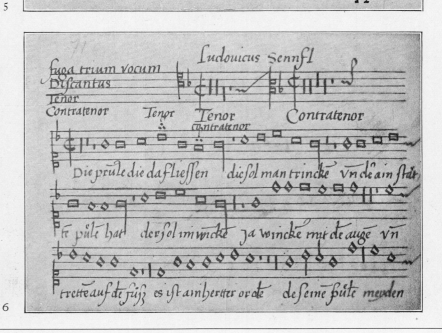

(**1**) Heinrich Finck (1445–1527); Hofkapellmeister at Cracow, Stuttgart, and Salzburg; as a composer, the most important contemporary of Heinrich Isaac. Medallion. London, British Museum. (**2**) and (**3**) Arnold von Bruck (d. 1554), Hofkapellmeister to the Emperor Maximilian I in Vienna, later in Munich; the greatest master of the German *lied* in the sixteenth century. Medallion by L. Neufarer, 1536. Vienna, Art History Museum. (**5**) Page a 2 from the *Chorale Constantinum* by Heinrich Isaac (d. 1517), a book of three-part motets published by his pupil Ludwig Senfl, Nuremberg, 1550, H. Formschneider. (**6**) *Die Brünnlein, die da fließen*, six-part song by Senfl (cf. fig. 4, p. 133). From the MS. song collection, year 1524. MS. 18810. Vienna, Nationalbibliothek.

(1) to (3) Musicians with bagpipe and rauschpfeife or shawm (discant bombard). Engravings by Hans Sebald Beham. (4) and (6) 'Pfeiffer' and 'Drumelschläger' (piper and drummer). Woodcuts by Beham (for Hanns Guldenmundt's Landsknechtfolge). (5) 'Der Sackpfeiffer' (the bagpiper). Engraving by Albrecht Dürer, 1514. (7) Three krummhorn (cromorne) players (1551). (8) Bass viol player (viola da gamba). Engraving by Albrecht Altdorfer. (9) Viol and lute players (1538). Engravings from the 'Hochzeitstänzer' series by Heinrich Aldegrever.

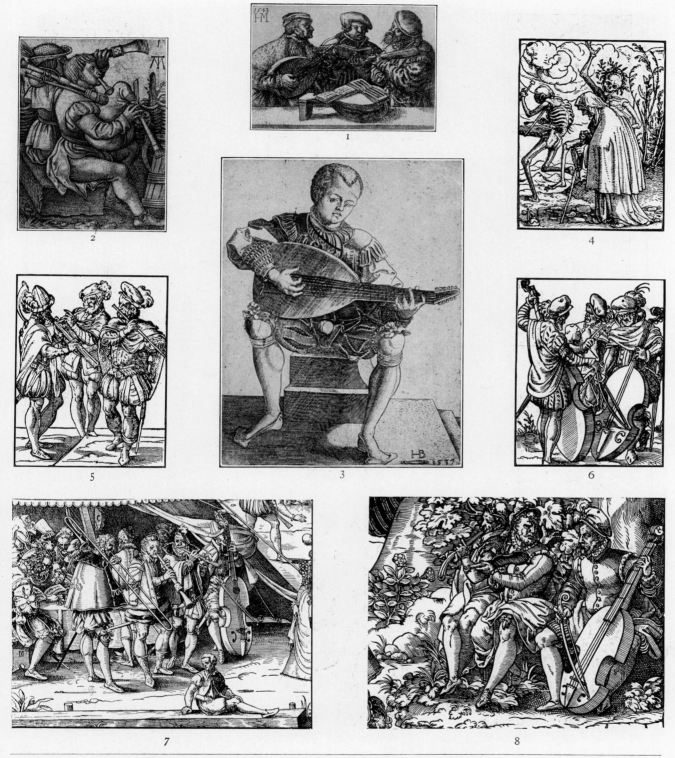

(1) Musicians (lutanist, singer, kit- [small fiddle-] player).   Engraving by the Master H. M., 1543.   (2) Musicians with bombard and bagpipe.   Engraving by the Master M[artin] T[reu].   (3) The lute player.   Engraving by Hans Brosamer, 1537.   (4) 'Old Woman.'   Death with the Holz- or Stroh-fiedel (xylophone), the so-called 'wooden laughter.'   Woodcut from the *Dance of Death* by Hans Holbein the Younger (*c.* 1525).   (5) Three wind players (straight and curved Zinke [cornets] and transverse flute).   (6) Three fiddlers (bass viols and small fiddle).   Woodcuts by Jost Amman from the *Beschreibung aller Stände, Künste und Handwerke* (with verses by Hans Sachs, Frankfort, 1568).   (7) and (8) Groups of musicians.   Woodcuts by Jost Amman from the so-called *Ehebrecherbrücke des Königs Artus.*

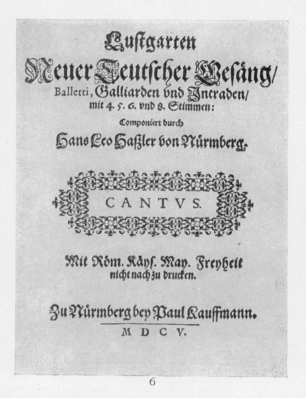

Hans Leo Hassler (1564–1612) was the greatest German composer of his age and the first German master to be educated in Italy (as a pupil of Andrea Gabrieli in Venice). (1) Portrait as organist to the Fuggers. Engraving by Domenico Custos, Augsburg, 1593. (2) and (3) Seal and signature from a receipted interest account in the name of the Fugger Brothers, Augsburg, 1594. Formerly in Cologne, Heyer Museum. (4) Jacob Handl (real name, Petelin), Lat.: Gallus (1550–91), leading composer of Catholic Church music in the sixteenth century. Engraving of 1590. (5) and (6) Title-pages to Hassler's motets (*Sacri Concentus*, Augsburg, 1601); and *Lustgarten neuer deutscher Gesänge*, Nuremberg, 1605 (second edition).

(1) Bernhard Schmid the Elder (1520-92): Two books of *Einer neuen künstlichen Tablatur auf Orgel und Instrument[en]*, Strasburg, 1577. B. Jobin. Title-page by Tobias Stimmer.   (2) Jacob Paix (1550-c. 1620) *Orgel Tablaturbuch*, Laugingen, 1583, L. Reinmichel.   Title-page after Tobias Stimmer.   (3) Bernhard Schmid the Younger (b. 1548): *Tabulaturbuch . . . auf Orgeln*, Strasburg, 1607, L. Zetzner.   Title-page by Hilarius Dieterlin.

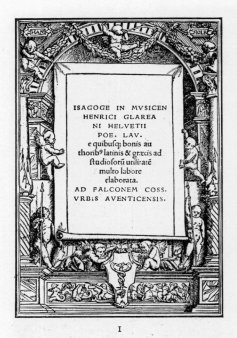

(**1**) Heinricus Glareanus (real name Heinrich Loris, 1488–1563): *Isagoge in musicen*, Basel, 1516.   Title-page by Hans Holbein the Younger.   (**2**) Georg Rhau (1488–1548): *Enchiridion musicae mensuralis*, Leipzig, 1520.   (**3**) Johann Frosch: *Rerum musicarum opusculum*, Strasburg, 1535.   Title-page by Hans Baldung Grien.   (**4**) Georg Rhau (see fig. 2 and p. 78), contemporary woodcut portrait.   (**5**) Adrian Petit Coclius (Netherlander, 1500–63, pupil of Josquin).   Woodcut portrait from the *Compendium musices*, Nuremberg, 1552.   (**6**) Sethus Calvisius (real name, Seth Kallwitz, 1556–1615).   Portrait. Engraving by Wolfgang Kilian, 1626.

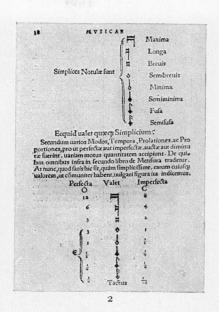

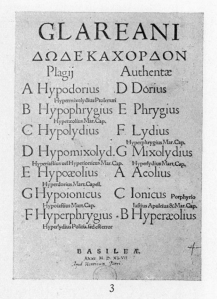

1

2

3

4   5

(**1**) Heinrich Faber (d. 1552): *Compendium musicae*, Nuremberg, 1548.   (**2**) Sebald Heyden (1498–1561): p. 38 of *Musicae id est artis canendi libri duo*, Nuremberg, 1537.   (**3**) Henricus Glareanus (see fig. 1, p. 84): *Dodekachordon*, Basel, 1547. (**4**) Adam Gumpelzhaimer (1559–1625). Portrait. Engraving by Lucas Kilian, 1662.   (**5**) The same: *Compendium musicae* (fifth edition), Augsburg, 1611.   Woodcut title-page, with concert of angels and muses.

(1) Hans Sachs (1494–1576), the Nuremberg shoemaker and poet, principal representative of the art of the Master-singers.   Portrait.   Engraving by Lucas Kilian (after Jost Amman), 1623.   (2) Hans Sachs: Einleitung zum eigenhändigen Liederbuch vom Jahre, 1552.   Dresden, Sächsische Landesbibliothek.   (3) Joh. Christoph Wagenseil (1633–1708), author of the book, *De civitate Noribergensi commentatio* (Altdorf, 1697), a work which Wagner used as a source of information on the guild of mastersingers.   Engraving by Jacob Sandrart, 1690.   (4) The Nuremberg mastersinger Wilhelm Weber. Engraving from the book by Wagenseil.

Four pages from a series of the nine muses. Tinted drawings by the Master S. M. in 1582. Similar in manner to the Swiss painter Christoph Maurer. (1) Positive organ; (2) lutes; (3) bass viol and rebec; (4) trumpets and trombones. Leipzig, Collection of Prints in the Städtische Museum.

1

2

3

4

5

(1) Adrian Willaert (c. 1485–1562), chapel-master of St. Mark's, Venice, from the end of 1527 and the founder of the Venetian school (see fig. 4). Engraving by L. C., Venice, 1559. (2) Filippo de Monte (1521–1603), imperial chapel-master under Maximilian II and Rudolf II, one of the most important composers of the *a cappella* age. Engraving by Raphael Sadeler. (3) Lambert de Sayve (1549–1614), court chapel-master to the emperor Matthias. Engraving from his *Sacrae symphoniae*, Helmstedt(?), 1612. (4) Adrian Willaert: Title-page to the *Musica nova* (collection of motets and madrigals), Venice, 1559, Ant. Gardano. (5) Jacob de Kerle (1531/32–91), one of the most distinguished of Orlando Lasso's contemporaries: title-page to *Quatuor missae* (choir-book). Antwerp, 1583. Christoph Plantin.

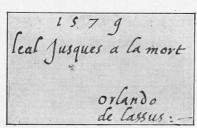

Orlando di Lasso (*c.* 1530–94), next to Palestrina the most famous composer of the sixteenth century, was Hofkapell-meister in Munich from 1560 onwards. (**1**) Unsigned woodcut dating from 1585. (**2**) Autograph album-leaf ('Faithful unto death') dating from 1579. Formerly in Cologne, Heyer Museum. (**3**) Engraving by René Boyvin. (**4**) Monument (Epithaphium) of the master, dating from 1595. Munich, Bayrisches Nationalmuseum. Museum photograph.

1

2

(1) Autograph letter of Lasso's to his patron Prince William [from 1579: Duke William V] of Bavaria, Friedberg, Munich, 18th May 1574. Munich, Geh. Hausarchiv. (2) Title-page to five-part masses, forming the second part of Lasso's greatest work, entitled *Patrocinium musices*, Munich, 1589, Adam Berg. Woodcut by I. N. [Johannes Nell]. In the lower space: Picture of an orchestra of nine instrumentalists and five singers. The five-volume *Patrocinium*, first published in 1573–6, is one of the finest pieces of music printing ever produced.

1

2

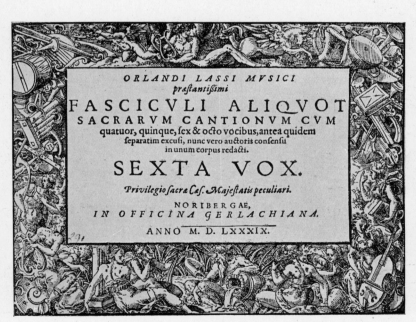

3   5   4

(1) to (4) From the MS.-Codex of 1565–70, containing Lasso's seven penitential Psalms of David (*Psalmi Davidis poenitentiales*), with beautiful illuminations by Hans Mielich (1516–73). Munich, Staatsbibliothek. (5) Title-page to an edition of Lasso's motets. Nuremberg, 1589, Katharina Gerlach.

1   2   3

4

(1) and (3) Lower-Rhenish masters: Two Dominicans playing positive organ and harp, 1501.   Vienna, Art History
Museum.   (2) Catharina van Hemessen: Self-portrait (at the spinet), 1543.   Cologne, Wallraf-Richartz Museum.
(4) Jacob Cornelisz van Oostanzen: Angels playing (discant shawms, dulcimer, busine, and trumpet), from the 'Birth of
Christ,' 1512.   Naples, Muzeo Nazionale.   Museum photographs.

(1) 'Music' (flute-à-bec; on the ground: portative organ, lute, harp, double flute, rebec). Florentine engraving, after the so-called 'Taroc cards of Mantegna,' ascribed to Baccio Baldini (c. 1470). Rotterdam, Museum Boijmans. (2) Landscape with two musicians (viola da braccio, bagpipe). (3) Shepherd blowing shawm. Engravings by Benedetto Montagna. (4) Amor with the three Graces (flutes-à-bec, viola da braccio). (5) The poet Philoletes of Bologna (Giov. Filoteo Achillini, 1466-1538) as guitar-player, after Franc. Francia. (6) Orpheus (with viola da braccio) and Eurydice. Engravings by Marc' Antonio Raimondi.

1

2

3

4

(**1**) William Cornysh, jun. (*c.* 1465–1523): three-part madrigal *Hoyda, jolly Rutterkin* in mensural notation (*c.* 1500). Add. MSS. 31922. (**2**) King Henry VIII (reigned 1509–47), well known as a patron of music, composer, and collector of instruments. Portrait of the king as harpist with his court jester William Sommers. Miniature from the Royal MS. 2 A XVI. (**3**) Page from the inventory made in 1547 of the king's collection of instruments. Harl. MS. 1419. (**4**) *Pastime with Good Company*, a three-part madrigal alleged to be the king's composition. Add. MSS. 31922; all in the British Museum.

I

2

3

(**1**) Mummers and musicians at the wedding feast of Sir Henry Unton.   Section of the unsigned painting representing scenes from the life of Sir Henry in the National Portrait Gallery, London.   Museum photograph.   (**2**) John Bull (1563–1628), organist of the Chapel Royal and a distinguished composer of organ and harpsichord music.   Oil portrait, painted in 1589.   Oxford, Music School.   (**3**) Hans Holbein the Younger: 'The Ambassadors,' Jean de Dinteville and Georges de Selve, Bishop of Lavour, ambassadors of Francis I of France to the English court, both patrons of music (lute, book of music, flute case).   Painted in 1533.   London, National Gallery.   Photograph by Bruckmann.

THE EXTRACT AND EFFECT OF THE QVENES
Maiesties letters patents to Thomas Tallis and VVilliam Birde,
for the printing of muficke.

ELIZABETH *by the grace of God Quene of Englande Fraunce and Irelande defender of the faith &c. To all printers bokefellers and other officers minifters and fubietts greting, Knowe ye, that we for the efpeciall affection and good wil that we haue and beare to the fcience of muficke and for the aduauncement thereof, by our letters patents dated the xxi1. of Ianuary in the xvi1. yere of our raigne, haue graunted full priuiledge and licence vnto our welbeloued feruaunts Thomas Tallis and VVilliam Birde Gent. of our Chappell, and to the ouerlyuer of them, & to the affignes of them and of the furuiuer of them, for xx1. yeares next enfuing, to imprint any and fo many as they will of fet fonge or fonges in partes, either in Englifh, Latine, French, Italian, or other tongues that may ferue for muficke either in Churche or chamber, or otherwife to be either plaid or foonge, And that they may rule and caufe to be ruled by impreffion any paper to ferue for printing or pricking of any fonge or fonges, and may fell and vtter any printed bokes or papers of any fonge or fonges, or any bookes or quieres of fuch ruled paper imprinted, Alfo we ftraightly by the fame forbid all printers bokefellers fubietts & ftrangers, other then as is aforefaid, to do any the premiffes, or to bring or caufe to be brought out of any forren Realmes into any our dominions any fonge or fonges made and printed in any forren countrie, to fell or put to fale, vppon paine of our high difpleafure, And the offender in any of the premiffes for euery time to forfet to vs our heires and fucceffors fortie fhllings, and to the faid Thomas Tallis & VVilliam Birde or to their affignes & to the affignes of the furuiuer of thẽ, all & euery the faid bokes papers fonge or fonges, VVe haue alfo by the fame willed & commaunded our printers, maifters & wardens of the mifterie of ftacioners, to affift the faid Thomas Tallis and VVilliam Birde & their affignes for the dewe executing of the premiffes.*

1

¶Reafons briefely fet downe by th'auctor, to perſwade
euery one to learne to fing.

First, it is a knowledge eaſely taught, and quickly learned, where
there is a good Maſter, and an apt Scoller.
  2   The exerciſe of finging is delightfull to Nature, & good
to preferue the health of Man.
3   It doth ſtrengthen all parts of the breſt, & doth open the pipes.
4   It is a finguler good remedie for a ſtutting & ſtamering in the
ſpeech.
5   It is the beſt meanes to procure a perfect pronunciation, & to
make a good Orator.
6   It is the onely way to know where Nature hath beſtowed the
benefit of a good voyce: which guift is fo rare, as there is not one among a thouſand, that hath it: and in many, that excellent guift is
loſt, becauſe they want Art to expreſſe Nature.
7   There is not any Muficke of Inſtruments whatſoeuer, comparable to that which is made of the voyces of Men, where the voices
are good, and the fame well ſorted and ordered.
8   The better the voyce is, the meeter it is to honour and ferue
God there-with: and the voyce of man is chiefely to be imployed
to that ende.

Omnis ſpiritus laudet Dominum.

Since finging is ſo good a thing,
I wiſh all men would learne to fing.

2

3

Royal patent for printing and selling music and music paper granted to Thomas Tallis (*c.* 1505–85) and William Byrd (1543–1623), composers and organists. From the *Cantiones sacrae*, London, 1575, Thomas Vautrollier. (**2**) Reasons for learning to sing, from the *Psalmes, Sonets, and Songs of Sadnes and Pietie* by William Byrd, London, 1558, Thomas Este. (**3**) John Dowland (1562–1626), composer and lute virtuoso. Autograph album-leaf (a fugue subject) for the *Album amicorum* of Johannes Cellarius of Nuremberg. Add. MSS. 27579, f. 88. London, British Museum.

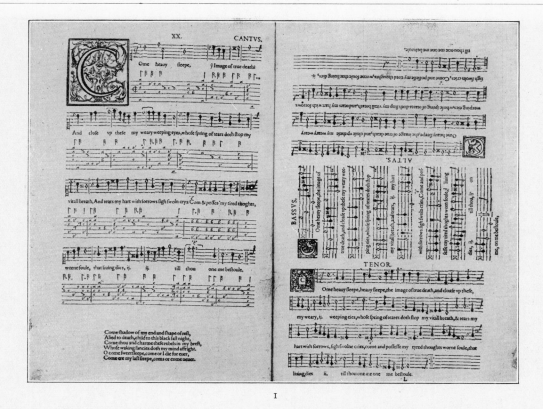

1

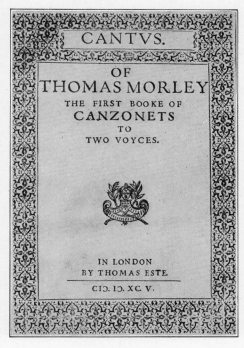

2

3

(1) John Dowland (1562–1626). From *The First Booke of Songes or Ayres of Foure Partes with Tableture for the Lute*, in French lute tablature (see p. 135). (The order of printing the parts corresponds to the grouping of the four singers and the lutanist round à table.) London, 1597, Peter Short. (2) and (3) Thomas Morley (1558–1603), highly esteemed composer of canzonets and madrigals. Title-page and leaf from *The first Booke of Canzonets to two voyces*, London, 1595, Thomas Este.

I

2

3

4

St. Filippo Neri (1515–95), founder, by permission of Pope Gregory XIII, of the *Congregazione dell'Oratorio* (1575) in which the art-form oratorio originated.   Unsigned engraving.   (**2**) View of the Sistine Chapel in Rome, built by Giovanni de' Dolci (1473–81).   Etching by Filippo Juvara, 1711.   (**3**) Title-page to the *Canticum Mariae Virginis* (Magnificat) by Giovanni Animuccia, Rome, 1568.   Heirs of V. and A. Dorico.   (**4**) Giovanni Animuccia (*c.* 1500–71), church composer, chapel-master of St. Peter's, Rome.   Oil portrait in the Liceo Musicale di Bologna (eighteenth century).

1

GIO: PIERLVIGI DA PALESTRINA

2

3

4

5

Giovanni Pierluigi da Palestrina (1525–94), the supreme master of Catholic church music (*Princeps musicae*). (**1**) Autograph record (after 1555) of the *Improperia* (Good Friday services). Extract from Codex 59 (the only preserved autograph volume containing the master's compositions) of the music archives of the Lateran in Rome. (**2**) Etching by Giuseppe Ghezzi (1711), after an oil painting of the sixteenth century in the papal chapel, Rome. (**3**) Signature from an autograph receipt, Rome, 18th March 1578. Formerly in the Heyer Museum, Cologne. (**4**) Woodcut on title-page of the first book of masses (Palestrina presenting the work to Pope Julius III). Choir-book, Rome, 1554, V. and A. Dorico. (**5**) From the first book of five-part madrigals, Venice, 1581, A. Gardano.

1

2

3

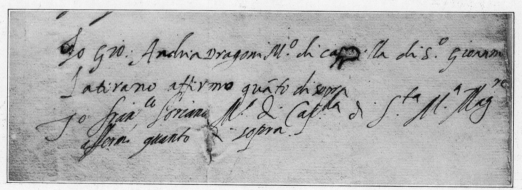

4

5

6

Palestrina's pupils, successors in office and so on: (**1**) Giovanni Maria Nanini (*c.* 1545–1607). Etching by Francesco Trevisani, 1711. (See also fig. 3, p. 153.) (**2**) Ruggiero Giovanelli (*c.* 1550–1625). Etching by P. de Petri, 1711. (**3**) Felice Anerio (1560–1614). Etching by F. A. P., 1711. (**4**) Marc' Antonio Ingegneri (*c.* 1545–92), teacher of Monteverde: autograph testimonial. Cremona, 11th December 1586. Formerly in the Heyer Museum, Cologne. (**5**) Francesco Soriano (1549–*c.* 1622). Oil painting in the Liceo Musicale di Bologna (eighteenth century). (**6**) Giovanni Andrea Dragoni (1540–98) and Francesco Soriano: autograph endorsements on a testimonial, Rome, 12th July 1595. Formerly in the Heyer Museum, Cologne.

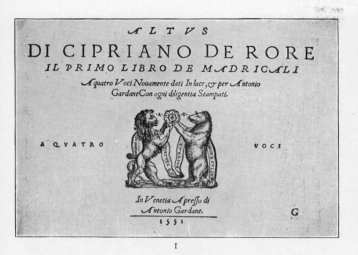

(1) Cipriano de Rore (1516–65).   Title-page to the first book of four-part madrigals, Venice, 1551, Antonio Gardano.
(2) Luca Marenzio (c. 1550–99), supreme master of the Italian madrigal.   Title-page to the first book of five-part madrigals, Venice, 1580, Angelo Gardano.   Madrigal-books of Palestrina and Monteverde (see fig. 4, p. 103, and fig. 3, p. 156).
(3) Sebastiano Florigerio: 'A Musical Entertainment' (c. 1540).   Munich, Alte Pinakothek.   Photograph by Hanfstaengl.

(1) Andrea Gabrieli (*c.* 1510–86), a pupil of Willaert (see fig. 1, p. 88), organist of St. Mark's, and a famous composer of organ and church music. *Mascherate*, Venice, 1601. (2) Andrea Gabrieli and Giovanni Gabrieli (1557–1612), his nephew and pupil, leader of the Venetian school and master of Heinrich Schütz. Title-page to the *Concerti* for voices and instruments, Venice, 1587. (3) Giovanni Gabrieli. *Sacrae symphoniae* (forty-five vocal and sixteen instrumental pieces), Venice, 1597. (4) Claudio Merulo (see p. 107). Title-page to two eight- and twelve-part masses, Venice, 1609; published, as were also 1 to 3, by Angelo Gardano.

(1) Cristobal Morales (*c.* 1500–53), eminent church composer. Six-part mass *Mille regrets* from *Missarum liber I*, Rome, 1544, V. and L. Dorico. (2) Miguel de Fuenllana, blind lutanist (*c.* 1550). Title-page to *Libro de musica para Vihuela, intitulado Orphenica lyra* (in tablature for the Spanish lute). Seville, 1554, M. de Montesdoca. (3) Don Antonio de Cabezon (1510–66), blind organist and composer. From the *Obras de musica para Tecla* (=key, keyed instrument), *Arpa y Vihuela* in Spanish organ tablature, Madrid, 1578, Franc. Sanchez. (4) Tomás Luis de Victoria (Vittoria, *c.* 1540–1613), chapel-master in Rome and Madrid, one of the finest masters of the Palestrina style. Title-page to a book of motets (*Cantiones sacrae*), Dillingen, 1589, Joh. Mayer.

1

2

3

4

(1) and (4) Society Dance and Peasants' Dance. Engravings by Jan Theodor de Bry (1561–1623). (2) Aristocratic dance couple. Engraving by Giac. Francho from the *Ballarino* of Caroso Fabritio, a work of great importance for the dance and costume lore of the late Italian Renaissance, Venice, 1581. (3) From the *Orchésographie* of Toinot Arbeau (Jean Tabourot, 1519–95), principal source for the study of sixteenth-century dancing. (*Métode, et Téorie en forme de discours et tablature pour apprendre à dancer.*) Second edition, Langres, 1596.

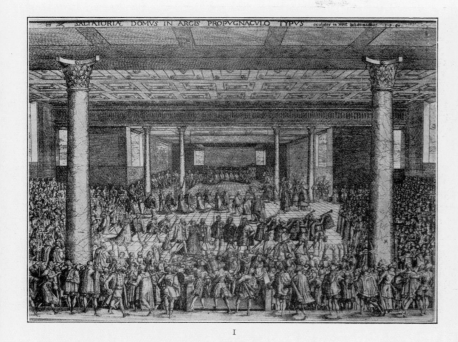

1

2

3

(**1**) Grand ball in the Hofburg, Vienna, in 1560. Etching by Francesco Terzi. (**2**) Dance Scene (p. 4 of a series). Engraving by Crispin van de Passe after Maerten de Vos. (**3**) Ball at the court of Henry III to celebrate the marriage of Duke Anne de Joyeuse and Princess Margarethe of Lorraine in 1851. (See fig. 1, p. 187.) Painting by the pupil of Floris, Herman van der Mast(?). Paris, Musée du Louvre. Museum photograph.

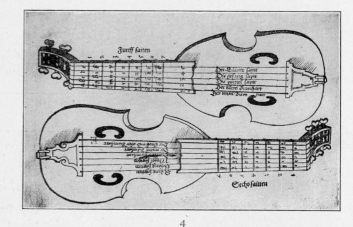

(1) to (3) Title-page and two others from *Musica getutscht* (i.e. verdeutscht [Germanized]) by the Amberg priest Sebastian Virdung, Basel, 1511, the oldest printed work on musical instruments. (See also fig. 1, p. 132.) Woodcuts by the Swiss artist Urs Graf; fig. 2 shows Virdung with his pupil Andreas Silvanus. (4) Illustration of bass viols from *Musica teutsch* by Hans Gerle, Nuremberg, 1532. (5) to (7) Title-page and two others from *Musica instrumentalis deudsch* by Martin Agricola (real name, Martin Sore, 1486–1556), Wittenberg, 1528–9, a revised edition of Virdung's *Musica getutscht* in doggerel verse with the same illustrations.

I   2

3

(1) Italian organ (positive) with the arms of the family della Rovere from which Pope Julius II (reigned 1503–13), was descended. First half of the sixteenth century. Leipzig, Heyer Collection. (2) Small positive organ of 1627 with the arms of the Elector Johann Georg I of Saxony (reigned 1611–56). London, Victoria and Albert Museum. (3) German positive of the seventeenth century combined with a so-called art chest. From the Ambras Collection, Art History Museum, Vienna. (Organ [positive] by Claudio Merulo; see fig. 3, p. 107.)

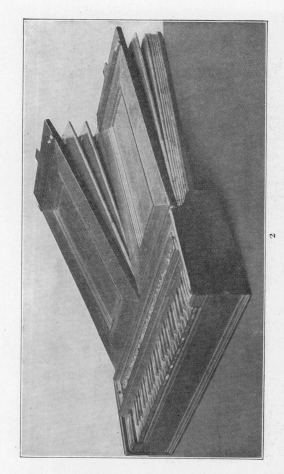

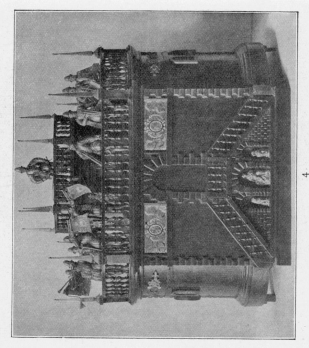

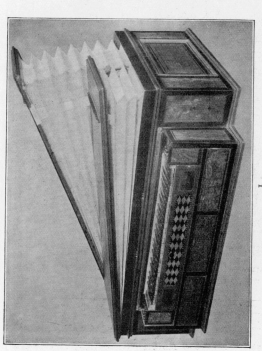

(1) Positive, laid flat. Tirol, first half of the seventeenth century. Leipzig, Heyer Collection.   (2) Regal organ (with beating-reeds and a quavering tone). Nuremberg, seventeenth century. Nuremberg, Germanic Museum.   (3) Claviorganum (organ with harpsichord) by Lodewyk Theeuwes, Antwerp, 1579. Formerly in the chapel of Ightham Mote, near Sevenoaks, Kent.   London, Victoria and Albert Museum.   (4) Trumpeter automaton with small regal built in.   South German (Augsburg?), second half of the sixteenth century.   Present from Duke William IV of Bavaria to his uncle the Archduke Ferdinand of Tirol, owner of the Ambras treasures.   Vienna, Art History Museum.

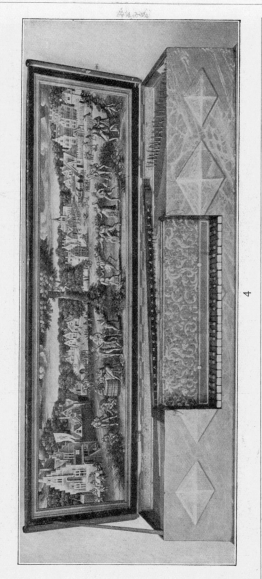

(1) Large double virginal made at Antwerp in 1580 by Martin van der Biest for the Stadthalter of the Netherlands, Alessandro Farnese (1547–92). Nuremberg, Germanic Museum. (2) Octave virginal; probably made by Hans Rückers the Elder, head of the famous Flemish family of piano-makers, at Antwerp (c. 1610). Leipzig, Heyer Collection. (3) Octave virginal. Flemish work (Antwerp) c. 1600, formerly in the Molenaer Collection. (4) Virginal made at Antwerp (c. 1580), by Jan Growuels (Grauwels), with a lid painted after the manner of Pieter Brueghel. Brussels, Musée du Conservatoire de Musique.

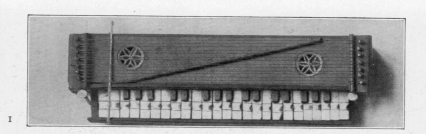

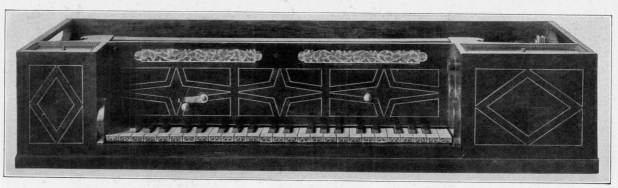

(**1**) Model of a clavichord of the late Middle Ages (tangent clavier), Germany, sixteenth century. Produced by the Ambrase Art Gallery. Vienna, Art History Museum. (**2**) Clavichord by Domenico da Pesaro (Dominicus Pisaurensis), Venice, 1543. Leipzig, Heyer Collection. (**3**) Inscription on the clavichord in fig. 2. (**4**) Clavichord (Netherland?), first half of the seventeenth century. Leipzig, Heyer Collection. (**5**) Octave virginal (small, rectangular spinet) bearing the arms of Duke William VI of Jülich-Cleve-Berg (reigned 1539–92). Netherlands, second half of the sixteenth century. London, Victoria and Albert Museum. (**6**) Automatic spinet set in a so-called cabinet (the mechanism worked by means of a roller with pins), by Samuel Bidermann, Augsburg. Second half of the sixteenth century. From Schloss Ambras. Vienna, Art History Museum.

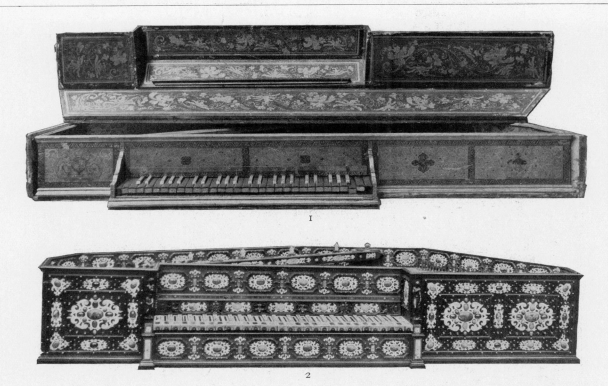

I

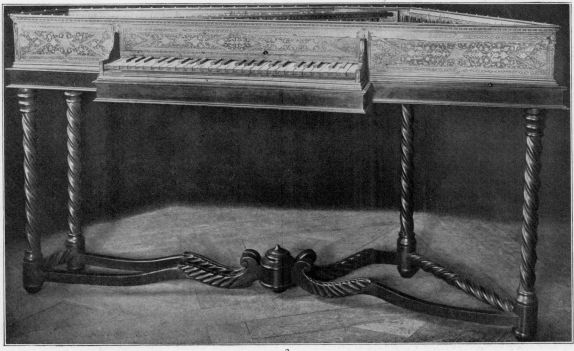

2

3

(1) Queen Elizabeth's virginal. Spinet belonging to Queen Elizabeth of England, who was a patroness of music (reigned 1558–1603). Italian, second half of the sixteenth century. London, Victoria and Albert Museum. (2) Spinet made by Annibale dei Rossi, Milan, 1577. This spinet, which is adorned with nearly 2,000 precious stones, is one of the most valuable instruments in the world. London, Victoria and Albert Museum. Acquired in 1867 from the Clapisson-Paris Collection for £1,200. (3) Spinet made by Giovanni Antonio Baffo, Venice, 1570. Paris, Musée de Cluny.

1

2

3

(**1**) Cembalo (Clavicembalo, Kielflügel) by Giovanni Antonio Baffo, Venice, 1574 (cf. fig. 3, p. 123). London, Victoria and Albert Museum. (**2**) Two-manual cembalo by Giovanni Pertici, Florence, 1683. Leipzig, Heyer Collection. (**3**) The piano-maker (cembalaro) Antonio Colonna. Portrait in oils in the Liceo Musicale di Bologna.

I

2

3

(**1**) Two-manual clavecin in Louis XIV style, the lid painted after the manner of Claude Lorrain.   France, seventeenth century.   Paris, Musée de Cluny.   (**2**) The Nuremberg violin mechanism ('Nürnbergisches Geigenwerk'), invented about 1575 by Hans Haiden of Nuremberg (the 'violinclavi-cymbel' or stringed piano).   Woodcut from *Syntagma Musicum* by Michael Praetorius, Wolfenbüttel, 1620 (cf. fig. 2, p. 164).   (**3**) Violin mechanism by Fray Raymundo Truchado, 1625, a Spanish imitation of Haiden's 'Nuremberg violin mechanism.'   Brussels, Musée du Conservatoire de Musique.

(**1**) and (**2**) Two pages from *Il Transilvano. Dialogo sopra il vero modo di sognar organi & istromenti da penna* by Girolamo Diruta (parts 1 and 2), Venice, 1597 and 1609; one of the most ancient books of instruction for the playing and fingering of keyed instruments.   (**3**) and (**4**) Title-page and page (with two pieces by William Byrd) from *Parthenia, or the Maydenhead of the first musicke that ever was printed for the Virginalls*, the first engraved collection of English piano music (with twenty-one pieces by William Byrd, John Bull, and Orlando Gibbons, in six-lined piano notation).   Engraved by William Hole. London, 1611, G. Lowe.

1

2

3

4

(1) In the style of Pieter Cornelisz van Slingelandt (or of his master Gerard Dou): 'The Music Lesson' (woman at the clavichord; right foreground: viola da gamba). Dresden Gallery. Reproduced by Bruckmann. (2) Jan Miensze Molenaer: Lady at the virginal. Amsterdam, Rijksmuseum. Reproduction by Hanfstaengl. (3) Eglon Hendrik van der Neer: Woman playing the zither in front of the virginal, 1669. Rotterdam, Boijmans Museum. Reproduction by the museum. (4) Frans van Mieris: Lady at the clavecin. 1658. Schwerin, Museum. Reproduction by the museum.

(1) Pandurina (mandola), France, second half of the sixteenth century.   London, Victoria and Albert Museum.   (2) Pandurina by Wendelin Tieffenbrucker, Padua (c. 1600).   Vienna, Art History Museum.   (3) Lute made of ivory, Venice,
early seventeenth century.   London, Victoria and Albert Museum.   (4) Lute (old, or choir-lute) by Laux Maller, Bologna
(c. 1520).   Vienna, Art History Museum.   Laux (Lucas) Maller was the earliest master of the art of lute-making, and,
like the majority of his fellow-artists in Northern Italy, was of German origin.   (5) Lute by Caspar Tieffenbrucker (cf.
fig. 5, p. 146), Lyons, c. 1560.   Berlin-Halensee, Wildhagen Collection.   (6) Lute by Wendelin Tieffenbrucker, Padua,
1582.   Vienna, Art History Museum.

1   2

3   4

(1) Tintoretto (Jacopo Robusti): 'The Lute Player.' Brunswick Gallery. (2) Judith Leyster (pupil of Frans Hals): 'The Serenade.' Amsterdam, Rijksmuseum (formerly: Galerie Six). (3) Jan Steen: Self-portrait of the artist as lute player. Formerly in London, Earl of Northbrook's Collection. (4) Anton van Dyck: 'The Lute Player.' Formerly in London, Earl of Northbrook's Collection. Reproductions by Bruckmann.

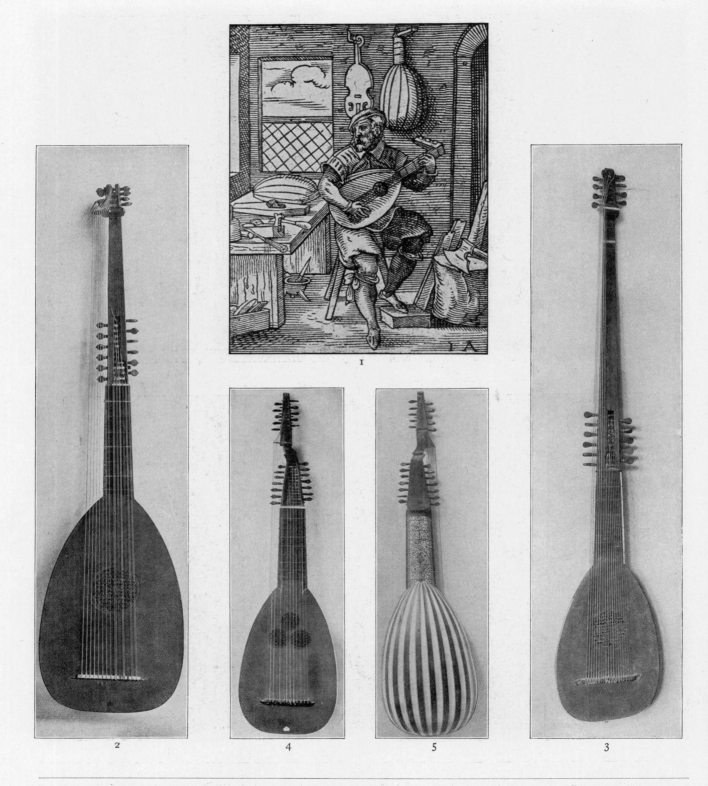

(1) 'The Lute Maker.'   Woodcut by Jost Amman, 1568 (see fig. 6, p. 81).   (2) Chitarrone (large bass- or arch-lute, 'Paduan theorbo') by Wendelin Tieffenbrucker, Padua, 1611.   Vienna, Art History Museum.   (3) Chitarrone by Michele Attore, Venice, 1620.   Leipzig, Heyer Collection.   (4) and (5) Theorbo (bass lute) bearing the name of Andrea Harton (Hartung), Venice, 1517.   (Back and front views.)   Berlin-Halensee, Wildhagen Collection.

1

2

3

(**1**) Theodor van Thulden: 'Amor and Music' (woman playing the so-called theorboed lute), 1662. Brussels, Musée de Peinture. Reproduction by the museum. (**2**) Caravaggio (Michelangelo Amerighi da C.). Man playing the chitarrone (on the table: tambourine, music book, and guitar) (*c.* 1590). Turin, Pinacoteca. Reproduction by Alinari. (**3**) Theodor Rombouts: Allegorical picture, 'The Five Senses,' showing a man playing the chitarrone (at his feet: bombard, two violins, lute, dolcian) (*c.* 1620). Ghent, Musée des Beaux Arts. Reproduction by museum.

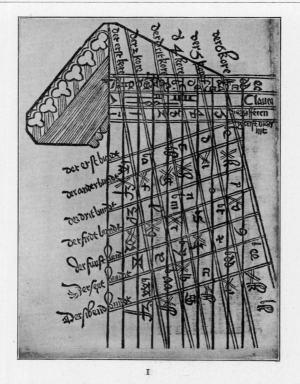

1

2

3

4

(1) Section of the fingerboard of a lute (with diagram showing the frets which determine the positions) from *Musica getutscht* by Sebastian Virdung, Basel, 1511 (see p. 118). (2) Title-page to *Ain schone Kunstliche vnderweisung—auff der Lautten vnd Geygen'* (instruction in the art of the lute and violin) by Hans Judenkünig (d. 1526), Vienna, 1523. (3) and (4) Title-page and portrait of the author from the *Tabulaturbuch auff die Lauten* (tablature for the lute) by Sebastian Ochsenkhun (1521–74), Heidelberg, 1558.

2

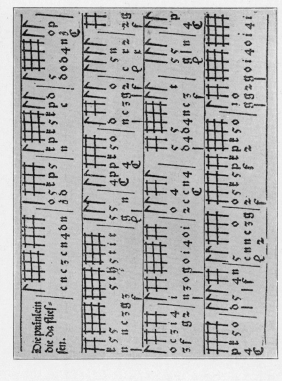

1

3

4

Lute books of the Nuremberg lutanist and lute-maker Hans Gerle (d. 1570): (1) Title-page to *Musica Teusch auf die Instrument der . . . Geygen auch Lautten*, Nuremberg, 1532 (cf. fig. 4, p. 118). (2) Title-page to *Tabulatur auff die Lautten* —, Nuremberg, 1533. (3) Song *Elslein, liebes Elslein*, from H. Gerle's *Musica vnd Tabulatur* (second edition), Nuremberg, 1546. (4) Song *Die Brünnlein, die da fließen* by L. Senfl (cf. fig. 6, p. 79), from *Ein Newgeordnet Künstlich Lautenbuch* by Hans Neusiedler (1508–9–63), Nuremberg. 1536. Figs. 3 and 4 are examples of the German tablature for the lute, an alphabetical notation in which the letters indicating the positions run in alphabetical order obliquely across the frets.

1

2

3

4

(1) Title-page to the first book *Newerlessner—Schöner Lautenstück* by Bernhard Jobin (d. *c.* 1590, brother-in-law of Johann Fischart), Strasburg, 1572. Woodcut by Tobias Stimmer (cf. fig. 1, p. 83). (2) Portrait of the lutanist Melchior Neusiedler (1507–90). Woodcut (1550) from the *Teutsch Lautenbuch*, Strasburg, 1574, Bernhard Jobin. (3) Title-page to *Intabolatura di Liuto* by Francesco da Milano, Venice, 1536. (4) Opening bars of *La bataglia*, from Francesco's lute book (fig. 3): Example of Italian tablature for the lute, in which the positions (frets) are indicated by figures on six lines corresponding to the strings; the top line represents the lowest string. (Spanish lute books of the sixteenth century: see fig. 2, p. 114 and fig. 2, p. 115.)

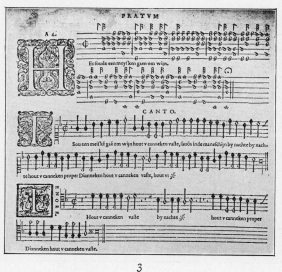

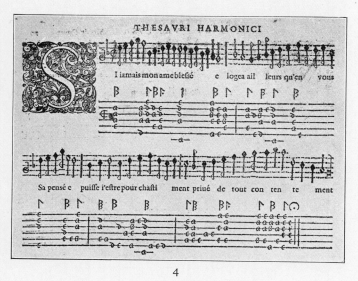

(1) Title-page to *Intavolatura de Leuto* by Jan Matelart, Rome, 1559, Val. Dorico. (Dedication copy. Formerly at Cologne, Heyer Museum.) (2) From the *Libro primo d'intavolatura di Chitarone* by Johann Hieronymus Kapsberger (d. *c.* 1650), Venice, 1604. (3) From the *Pratum Musicum* by Emanuel Adriaensen (Hadrianius Antverpiensis), Antwerp, 1584, Pierre Phalèse. (4) From the *Thesaurus Harmonicus* by Jean Baptiste Besard, Cologne, 1603, G. Grevenbroich. Figs. 3 and 4: Examples of the French tablature for the lute in which the positions are indicated by letters (instead of figures as in the Italian tablature), and the top line represents the highest string.

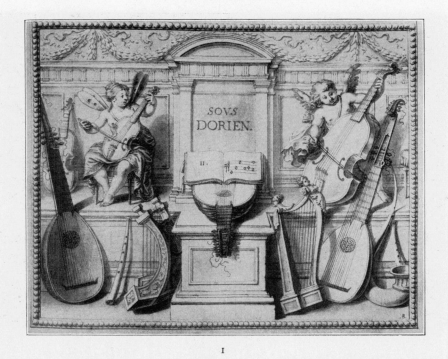

I

2

3

(**1**) A title-page from the manuscript collection of pieces by Denis Gaultier known as *La Rhétorique des Dieux*.　Indian ink drawing by Abraham Bosse (*c.* 1665).　Codex Hamilton in the collection of engravings at Berlin.　(**2**) Jacques Gaultier (Gautier) the Elder, Sieur de Neüe (*c.* 1600–70), English court lutanist.　Drawing by Jan Lievens.　(**3**) Portrait of a lutanist (chitarronist) said to be the famous lute virtuoso Denis Gaultier the Younger (*c.* 1605–72).　Picture by Anton van Dyck.　Madrid, Museo del Prado.　Reproduction by Anderson.　(See also fig. 1, p. 139.)

1

2

3

4

(**1**) Title-page to *Regola Rubertina* by Silvestro Ganassi dal Fontego (cf. fig. 1, p. 148), Venice, 1542, a book of instructions in the playing of the viola da gamba, dedicated to the statesman Roberto Stozzi.   The only copy known to exist; in the Liceo Musicale di Bologna.   (**2**) Title-page to *Trattado de Glosas . . . en la Musica de Violines* by the Spaniard Diego Ortiz, Rome, 1553; a book of instructions in the playing of variations on the viole da gamba.   Copy in the Staatsbibliothek, Berlin.   (**3**) Domenichino (Domenico Zamperi): Saint Cecilia playing a seven-stringed bass viola da gamba (*c.* 1620). Paris, Louvre.   Photograph by Alinari.   (**4**) Caspar Netscher: Musical entertainment, woman playing the tenor viola da gamba: French, basse de viole (*c.* 1670).   Formerly at The Hague, in the Steengracht Collection.   (Copy after the painting in the Louvre.)   Photograph by Bruckmann.

(**1**) Miniature violin (Trögl, pochette, kit, or pocket fiddle).   Germany, fifteenth to sixteenth centuries?   Vienna, Figdor Collection.   (**2**) Fiddle (viola da braccio).   Italian (*c.* 1500).   Unique example.   Vienna, Art History Museum.   (**3**) Violin by Ventura Linarolo, Venice, 1581 (cf. fig. 3, p. 142, and fig. 5, p. 144), one of the oldest dated violins.   Vienna, Art History Museum.   (**4**) Violin with the English Royal Arms at the base of the neck.   Said to have belonged to James I of England (reigned 1603–25).   England, early seventeenth century.   London, Victoria and Albert Museum.   (**5**) The violin and lute maker Caspar Tieffenbrucker (Gaspar Duioffoprugcar, 1514–71; cf. fig. 5, p. 128).   Etching by Pierre Woeiriot, 1562.   (**6**) Violoncello having the arms of the ducal family of d'Este on the richly carved back.   Italian, sixteenth century.   Modena, Galeria Estense.

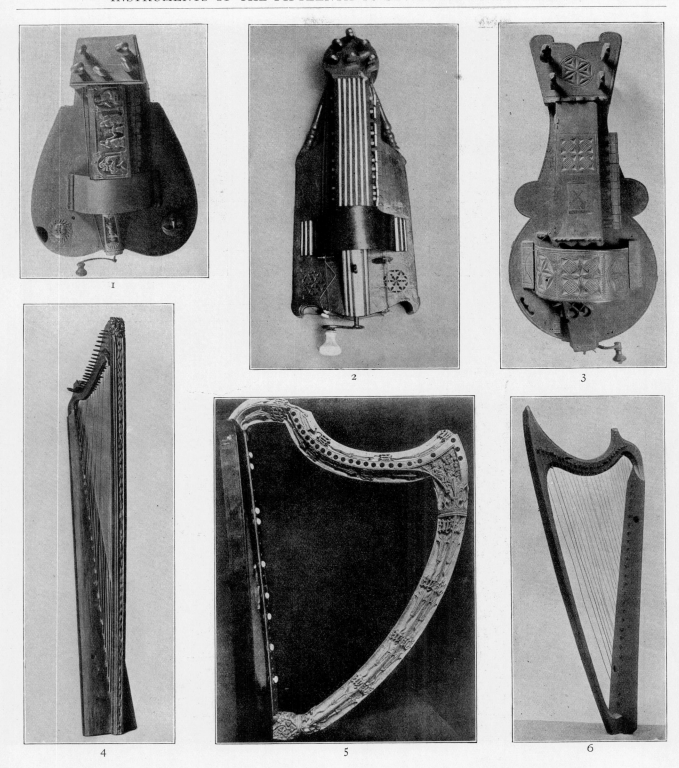

(1) Hurdy-gurdy (German: Radleier, Drehleier, beggar's or peasant's lyre. French: vielle). Germany, sixteenth century. Nuremberg, Germanic Museum. (2) Vielle bearing the monogram of Henry II of France (reigned 1549–57) and of his queen, Catharine of Medici. France, sixteenth century. London, Victoria and Albert Museum. (3) Hurdy-gurdy. Germany, early seventeenth century. Berlin-Halensee, Wildhagen Collection. (4) Harp branded with 'G. M.' Italian, sixteenth century. Vienna, Art History Museum. (5) Harp (harpe portative), with Gothic carving. France, fifteenth century. Paris, Louvre. (6) Harp of Gothic design. Germany, fifteenth to sixteenth centuries. Nuremberg, Germanic Museum.

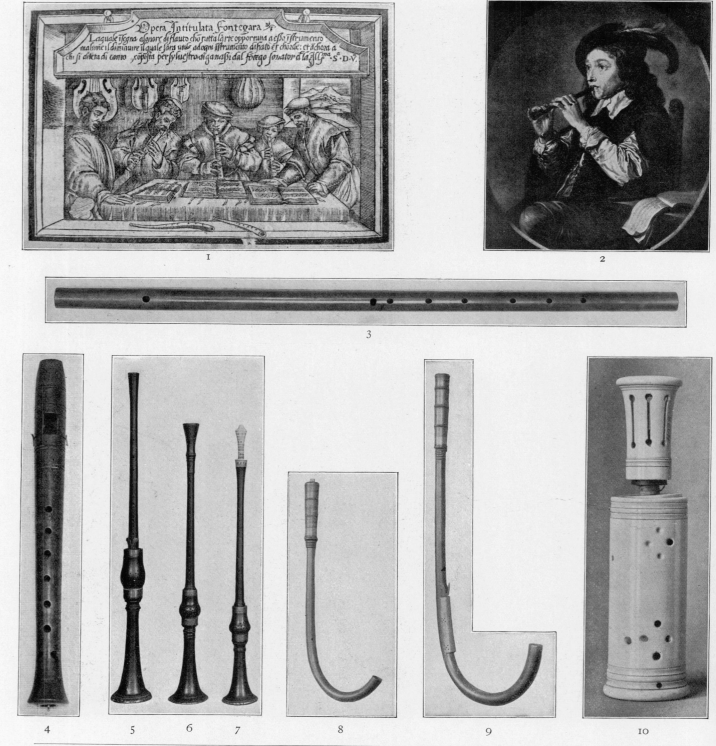

(**1**) Title-page to *Opera intitulata Fontegara* by Silvestro Ganassi (cf. fig. 1, p. 145), Venice, 1535; instructions in the playing of the flute-à-bec (Blockflöte).   (**2**) The flautist (flute-à-bec).   Drawing by Johann V. Kauperz after the painting by Gerard Dou in the Ferdinandeum Museum, Innsbruck.   (**3**) German flute (Querflöte).   (**4**) Small, sixteenth-century flute-à-bec.   Vienna, Art History Museum.   (**5**) to (**7**) Alto bombard; shawm (descant bombard); Poitou shawm.   Seventeenth century.   Leipzig, Heyer Collection.   (**8**) and (**9**) Alto and bass curved horns of the sixteenth century.   Leipzig, Heyer Collection.   (**10**) Ivory descant racket (fagot, of cylindrical design, known in German as 'Wurst' or sausage-fagot, and in France as 'Cervelas').   Tirol, late sixteenth century; from the Ambras Art Collection.   Vienna, Art History Museum.

1

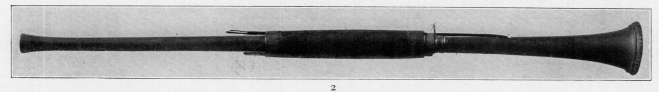

2

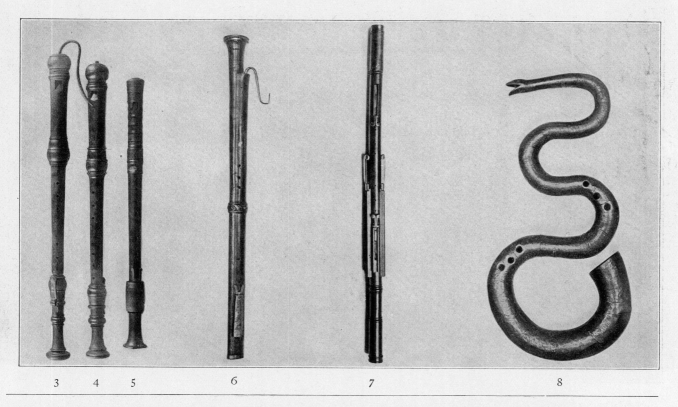

3   4   5   6   7   8

(**1**) Procession of musicians (dolcian, three bombards, curved cornet, trombones) from 'La procession des Pucelles du Sablon' by Antoine Sallaert (*c.* 1620).   Brussels, Musée de Peinture.   (**2**) Bass bombard by M.H., 1600.   Nuremberg, Germanic Museum.   (**3**) to (**5**) Bass flute-à-bec of the seventeenth century.   Nuremberg, Germanic Museum.   (**6**) Dolcian (double fagot, quadruple fagot) by Hier. S.   (**7**) Double bass sordino.   (**8**) Serpent (bass cornet in serpent form).   6, 7, and 8 date from the sixteenth century and are in the Art History Museum at Vienna.

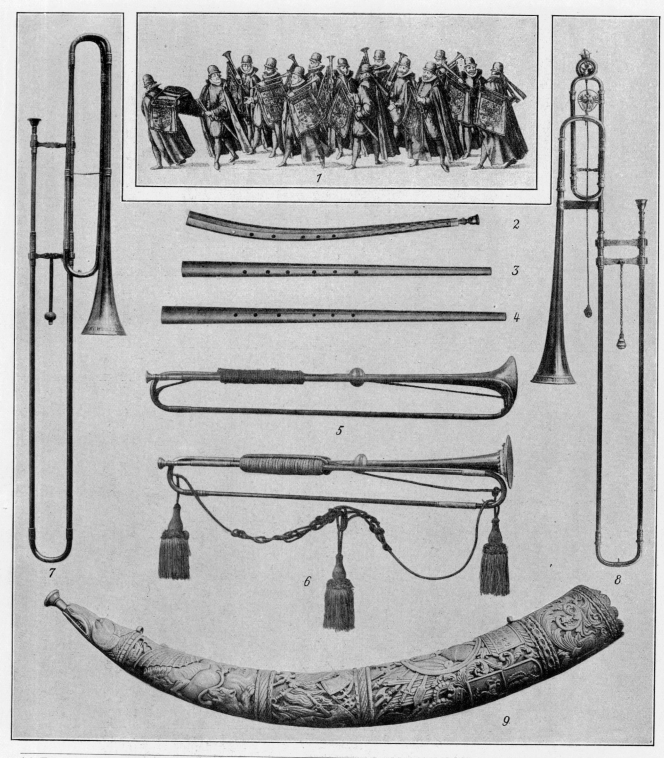

(1) Emperor Charles V's trumpeters in a funeral procession (Brussels, December 1558). Engraving by J. and L. van Duetecom after Jeremy Cock, from *Pompe funèbre de Charles V*, printed by Chr. Plantin at Antwerp, 1559. (2) Curved cornet (choir cornet). (3) and (4) Two 'cornetti muti'; sixteenth century. Leipzig, Heyer Collection. (5) and (6) Two trumpets by Joh. Carl Kodisch, Nuremberg, late seventeenth century. Nuremberg, Germanic Museum. (7) Trombone by Pierre Colbert, Reims, 1593. Amsterdam, Rijksmuseum. (8) Octave, or double trombone (contrabass trombone) by Isaac Ehe, Nuremberg, 1612. Nuremberg, Germanic Museum. (9) Oliphant (ivory horn) owned by King John Sobieski of Poland (reigned 1674–96). Late seventeenth century. Wiesbaden, private collection.

Jan Brueghel (Velvet Brueghel): Picture 'Hearing' (showing a large number of the instruments in use in the early seventeenth century). From a series of allegorical paintings representing the Five Senses (c. 1620). Madrid, Museo del Prado. Photograph by Anderson.

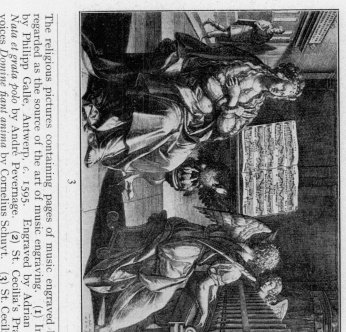

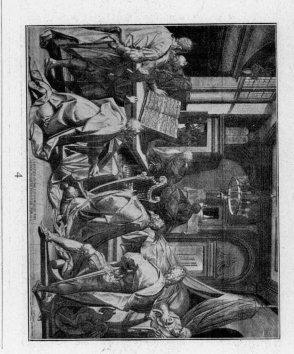

The religious pictures containing pages of music engraved by Johann Sadeler and other Antwerp engravers (from 1584 onwards) may be regarded as the source of the art of music engraving. (1) In Praise of Music. Title-page to the book of plates *Encomium Musices* published by Philipp Galle, Antwerp, *c.* 1595. Engraved by Adrian Collaert, after Jan van der Straet (Stradanus). Music: Motet for six voices *Nata et grata polo* by André Pevernage. (2) St. Cecilia's Prayer. Engraved by Zacharias Dolendo, after J. de Gheyn. Music: Motet for six voices *Domine fiant anima* by Cornelius Schuyt. (3) St. Cecilia's Prayer. Engraved by Johann Sadeler, after Martin de Vos. Music: Motet for five voices, *Fiat cor meum* by Dirk Raymundi. (4) King David at Prayer. Engraved by Johann Sadeler, after Jodocus van Winghe. Music: Motet for five voices, *Laude pia Dominum* by André Pevernage.

1

2

3

4

Simone Verovio of Rome was the first music publisher to make use of copper-plate engraving for music books; in this he was assisted (from 1586) by the Dutch engraver Martin van Buyten. (1) Page 19 from Book I of *Melodie spirituali a 3 voci* by Jacob Peeters (Peetrin), Rome, 1586; Verovio's first publication. The only known copy is in the Royal Library at Brussels. (2) and (3) Two pages from the collection *Diletto spirituale, Canzonette a 3 et a 4 voci*, Rome, 1586. Fig. 2: Canzonette *Spiega mondo Maligno* by Luca Marenzio, master of the art of the madrigal (see fig. 1, p. 105). Fig. 3: Motet *Jesus in pace imperat* by Giovanni M. Nanini (see fig. 1, p. 104), in Italian tablature for cembalo and lute. (4) Page 1 of *Arie devote* by Ottavio Durante, Rome, 1608.

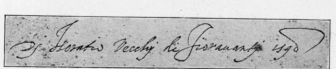

(1) Apollo's fight with the Pythian dragon.   Third interlude at the marriage feast of Ferdinand of Medici with Princess Christine of Lorraine (Florence, 1589).   Etching by Carraci, after Buontalenti.   Poem by Ottavo Rinuccini, music by Luca Marenzio (printed 1591).   In these interludes (intermezzi), which were still written in madrigal style, the musicians who were later to be the founders of the *Stilo rappresentativo o recitativo* and of the opera as an art form, first came before the public.   (2) Engraved frontispiece to the *commedia harmonica* (i.e. operetta) *l'Amfiparnasso* by Orazio Vecchi (*c.* 1550–1605), Venice, 1597, an important precursor of the first operas, also written in madrigal style.   (3) Signature of O. Vecchi (1598).   Formerly at Cologne, Heyer Museum.   (4) Title-page of the first libretto, *La Dafne*, poem by Ottavio Rinuccini, music by Jacopo Corsi, Florence, 1600, G. Marescotti.   (This earliest opera, with the music by Jacopo Peri, was produced in Count Giovanni Bardi's house at Florence in 1597.)

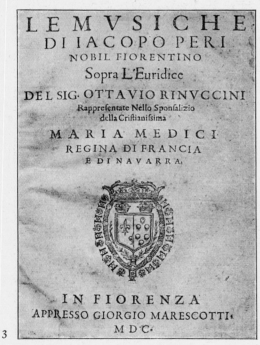

(**1**) Title-page of the libretto of the opera *Euridice*, composed by J. Peri and G. Caccini.   The libretto by Ottavio Rinuccini, Florence, 1600, C. Giunti.   (**2**) and (**3**) The two earliest printed opera scores.   (**2**) Woodcut for the score of *Euridice*, by Giulio Caccini detto Romano, dedicated to Count Bardi (*c.* 1545–1618), Florence, 1600, G. Marescotti.   (**3**) Title-page of the score of *Euridice*, by Jacopo Peri, dedicated to Queen Marie of France (1561–1633), Florence, 1600, G. Marescotti. Peri's work was performed, several pieces of Caccini being introduced, on 6th October 1600, on the occasion of the betrothal of King Henry IV of France with Maria dei Medici.   Caccini's composition, with the same libretto, was produced at Florence on 5th December 1602.   (**4**) Title-page of *Le varie musiche*, by Jacopo Peri, Florence, 1609, C. Marescotti. This work, like G. Caccini's *Nuove musiche*, of 1601, is an early example of the new, epoch-making, monodic style, which consisted in the union of a single voice with supporting instrumental thorough-bass parts.

1

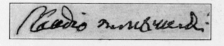

2

3

4

5

Claudio Monteverdi (1567–1643), the first great master of operatic music, was appointed choir-master of the church of St. Mark, in Venice, in the year 1613. (1) Portrait after the woodcut on the title-page of the compilation, *Fiori poetice . . . nel funerale del . . . Monteverde*, by Giov. Batt. Marinoni, Venice, 1644. (2) Signature of a letter written in Venice in 1630. Formerly in Cologne, Heyer Museum. (3) Title-page of the second volume of madrigals for five voices, Venice, 1590, Ang. Gardano. (4) Title-page of the score of the opera *Orfeo*, dedicated to Don Francesco Gonzaga (libretto by Aless. Striglio the Elder), Venice, 1609, Ricc. Amadino. First performance, Mantua, 1607. (5) Etching for the title-page of the libretto of the opera *La Flora*, Florence, 1628. Libretto by Andrea Salvadori. Music by Marco da Gagliano (c. 1575–1642). Etching by Alfonso Parigi.

(1) 'La guerra d'amore,' allegorical festival on the Piazza S. Croce at Florence, 1615. Processions and tilting, with music by J. Peri, P. Grazi, and G. B. Signorini, scenery by G. Parigi. Etching by Jacques Callot. (2) 'Il mondo festeggiante,' tilting festival (Balletto a cavallo), at the marriage of the Grand Duke Cosimo III with Marguérite Louise of Orleans; Florence, 1661. Text by G. A. Moniglia, music by Domenico Anglesi. Etching by Stefano della Bella.

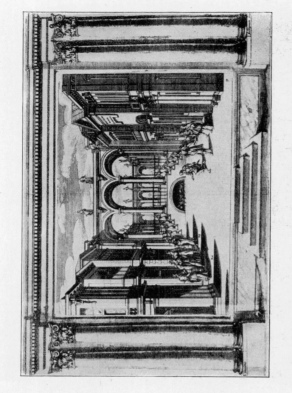

2

4

1

3

(1) Camp scene from the opera *Erminia sul giordano*, Rome, 1633.   (For the opening of the Teatro Barberini.)   Libretto by Giulio Rospigliosi, afterwards Pope Clement IX; music by Michelangelo Rossi; scenery by Franc. Guitti.   (2) Domestic scene from the sacred opera *Sant' Alessio*, Rome, 1634. Libretto by Giulio Rospiglioso; music by Stefano Landi; scenery by the architect and sculptor Lorenzo Bernini.   (3) Entrance of Mars from *L'Ermione*, Padua, 1636.   Libretto by Pio Enea degli Obizzi; music by Felice Sances; scenery by Alf. Chenda.   (4) Conflagration scene from *Ercole in Jebe*, Florence, 1661 (see fig. 2, p. 157).   Libretto by G. A. Moniglia; music by Jacopo Melani.   Etching by Valerio Spada.

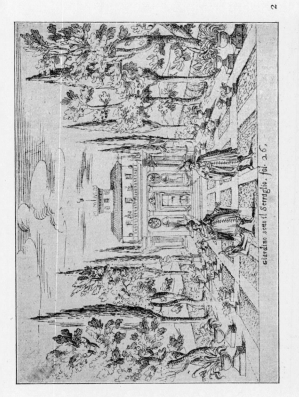

2

4

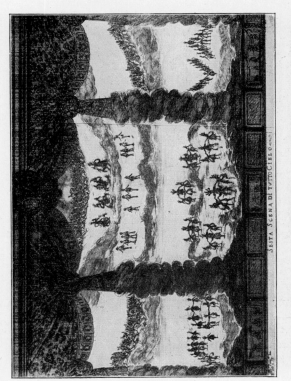

1

3

(1) Celestial scene from the *Favola*, 'Le nozze degli Dei,' Florence, 1637. Libretto by G. C. Coppola, music by. Marco da Gagliano and four other composers; scenery by Alf. Parigi. Etching by Stefano della Bella. (2) Harem scene from the opera *La Dori*, Florence, 1661, and Venice, 1663. Libretto by Apoll. Apolloni; music by Marc' Antonio Cesti. Etching by S. M. (from the text published 1665 in Macerata). (3) View of a town from the opera *L'età dell' oro*, Parma, 1690. Libretto by L. Lotti; music by Giuseppe Felice Tosi; scenery by Ferdinando Galli Bibiena. Engraving by Martial Desbois. (4) Last scene of the opera *Il favore degli Dei*, Parma, 1690. Libretto by Aurelio Aureli; music by Bernardo Sabadini; scenery by Ferdinand Galli Bibiena and the brothers P. D. and G. Mauro. Engraving by Dom. Bonavera, after Domenico Mauro.

(1) Title-page of the first (and only) book of instrumental preludes by Alessandro Orlogio (Dresden), Helmstädt, 1597. An early example of pure instrumental music.   (2) Title-page of the mass for eight voices by Camillo Cortellini (Bologna), Venice, 1617.   (3) Title-page of the third book of sonatas, etc., by Salomone Rossi (Mantua), Op. 12, Venice, 1623. An early example of the trio sonatas (for two violins with bass and cembalo), which were still in great favour in the eighteenth century.   The only known copy is in the Town Library of Breslau.   (4) Title-page of the clavier and organ toccatas of Girolamo Frescobaldi (see p. 161), Rome, 1637.

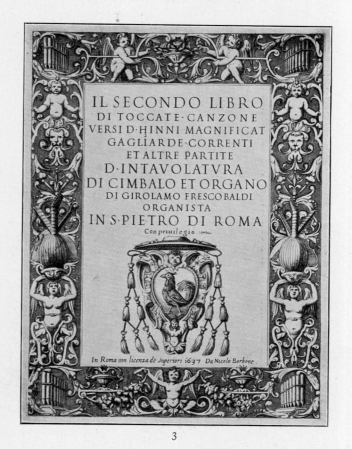

Girolamo Frescobaldi (1583–1643), the most important and most distinguished Italian organist and composer of his time.   From 1608 onwards, he was organist of St. Peter's Church, Rome.   Joh. Jacob Froberger, organist at the court of Vienna, was one of his pupils. (**1**) Portrait. Engraving by Christian Sas from the first volume of *Toccate e Partite d'intravolatura di Cimbalo*, Rome, 1614–16, Nic. Borbone. (**2**) Page 1 of the same work (in Italian clavier or organ tablature. Music engraving). (**3**) Engraved title-page from the second volume of *Toccate Canzone . . . et altre Partite d'intravolatura di Cimbalo ed Organo*, Rome, 1637, Nic. Borbonne. (**4**) Signature of a letter written in Milan, 1608. Formerly in Cologne, Heyer Museum.

(1) Adriano Banchieri (c. 1565–1634), organist, theorist, and composer in Bologna.   (2) Alessandro de Grandi (d. 1630), composer of church music of the Venetian school in Venice and Bergamo.   (3) Steffano Landi (c. 1590–1655), one of the creators of the cantata and the first exponent of Roman opera (Padua, Rome).   (4) Giovanni Legrenzi (1626–90), one of the most important seventeenth-century composers of Northern Italy (Bergamo, Venice).   (5) Gregorio Allegri (1582–1652), singer in the papal choir and composer of church music in Rome, known for his *Miserere* for nine voices.   Engraving 1711.   (6) Giacomo Predieri (d. c. 1695), organist and choir-master in Bologna. (7) Giov. Paolo Colonna (1636–95), composer of church music and one of the founders of the Accademia Filarmonica at Bologna.   (8) Bernardo Pasquini (1637–1710), organist, vocal and instrumental composer (for the clavier) in Rome.   (Authenticity of the portrait uncertain.)   (9) Francesco Antonio Pistocchi (1659–1726), operatic composer and founder of the School of Singing at Bologna.   Figs. 1–4, 6, 7, and 9, mostly after eighteenth-century portraits in oils in Liceo Musicale of Bologna.

(1) Giovanni Battista Doni (1594–1647), research worker on Greek music and inventor of the Lyra Barberina.   Engraving by Vinc. Franceschini, after Giov. Dom. Feretti.   (2) Athanasius Kircher, Jesuit father (1602–80), authority on acoustics, writer on music and founder of the Museo Kircheriano at Rome.   Engraving dated 1664.   (3) Title-page to the *Musica practica* of Johann Andreas Herbst (1588–1666), Nuremberg, 1642; one of the first Singing Methods.   (4) Engraved title-page of the *Mechanica hydraulico-pneumatica* of the Jesuit father, Caspar Schott (1608–66), Frankfort, 1657.

1

2

3

(1) Portrait of Michael Praetorius (1571–1621), conductor of the orchestra to the court of Saxony. The greatest master of Protestant church music, and the most distinguished writer on music of his time. Woodcut dated 1606. (2) Frontispiece woodcut (representation of a mass sung by three choirs), to the *Theatrum instrumentorum seu Sciagraphia*, Wolfenbüttel, 1620. Index with a 'catalogue of almost every musical instrument'—for the second part of *Syntagma musicum*, by Praetorius (published 1615–20), the chief source of information on music, and on the instruments of the period (1600). (See also fig. 2, p. 125.) (3) Song, *Auf eine Jungfrau säuberlich*, from the *New Preludes . . . for Instruments, chiefly for Viols* (thirteen songs and thirty-one preludes by Valentin Hausmann, flourished c. 1580–1610). Nuremberg, 1604.

(1) Erasmus Widmann (1572–1634), cantor and composer at Rothenburg. Engraving from the *New Sacred Motets*, Nuremberg, 1619.   (2) Title-page to the *New Musical Preludes . . . especially for Viols*, by Melchior Franck (1573–1639), musician to the ducal court of Coburg. Nuremberg, 1608. (3) Johann Staden (1581–1634), organist and composer at Nuremberg. Engraving by Johann Pfann, 1640.   (4) Michael Altenburg (1584–1640), deacon and composer of church music at Erfurt. Woodcut dated 1621.

1

2

3

4

5

Heinrich Schütz (1585–1672), the greatest German composer of the seventeenth century, especially in the province of Protestant church music. From 1617 until his death he was court musician to the court of Saxony at Dresden. (1) Portrait. Engraving (in the year of the master's death) by Christian Romstet. (2) Title-page to the Passion Music, *History of the . . . Resurrection . . . of Jesus Christ*, Dresden, 1623. (3) Title-page to the third part of the *Symphoniae Sacrae* (sacred concerti for voices and instruments in the style of his master, Giovanni Gabrieli), Op. 12, Dresden, 1650. (4) Imprint ('Signum Gardani') from the title-page to the first part of *Symphoniae Sacrae*, Venice, 1629. (5) Signature of a memorandum to Prince Johann Georg I of Saxony, on the reform of the court orchestra, Dresden, 7th March 1641. Dresden, Saxon state archives. Libretto of the opera *Daphne*, 1627. (See fig. 1, p. 181.)

1   2   3

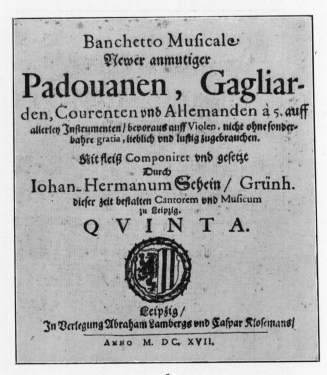

4   5

(**1**) Johann Hermann Schein (1586–1630), one of the greatest German masters of the first half of the seventeenth century. From 1616 onwards cantor of the Thomas Schule. Woodcut from the *Venuskränzlein*, Wittenberg, 1609. (See fig. 4.) (**2**) Johann Andreas Herbst (1588–1666), conductor in Darmstadt, Frankfort, and Nuremberg, composer and theorist. (See fig. 3, p. 163.) Engraving by Sebastian Fürck, 1635. (**3**) Heinrich Scheidemann (1596–1663), organist (pupil of J. P. Sweelinck) and composer at Hamburg. Engraving by J. F. Fleischberger, 1652. (**4**) and (**5**) Title-pages to two important works by J. H. Schein: *Venuskränzlein* (*Crown of Venus*) . . . *or new Secular Songs*, Wittenberg, 1609; *Banchetto Musicale* (*Musical Bouquet*) . . . *New Pavans, Galliards* . . . *on all kinds of instruments* (twenty suites in variation form), Leipzig, 1617.

(1) Engraved title-page to the first volume of *Preussischen Festlieder* by Eccard and Stobäus, Elbing, 1642. This work, Eccard's most important composition, was edited by Stobäus, after the death of the composer. (2) Johannes Eccard (1553–1611), the most distinguished North German composer of church music of his time. Choir-master at Königsberg and at Berlin. Engraving by Joh. Hermann from the *Preussischen Festlieder*, 1642 (see fig. 1). (3) Johannes Stobäus (1580–1646), pupil of Eccard, cathedral cantor and musician to the archducal court of Königsberg. Engraving by Joh. Hermann (see fig. 1).   (4) Engraved title-page to the first volume of *Arias or Melodies . . . some Sacred, some Secular Songs* by Heinrich Albert (1604–51), Königsberg, 1638.

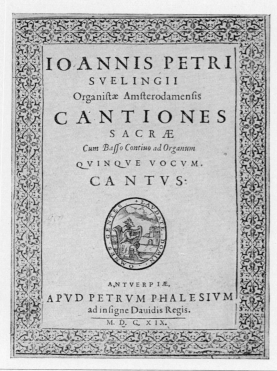

Jan Pieters Sweelinck (1562–1621), the Dutch master and pioneer of composition for the organ, and of organ playing, the so-called 'Maker of Organists.' Among his pupils were Sam. Scheidt, H. Scheidemann, Paul Siefert, and others. (1) Portrait. Engraving by Jan Müller, 1624. (2) Title-page to a book of motets for five voices, *Cantiones Sacrae*, Antwerp, 1619, Pierre Phalèse. Samuel Scheidt (1587–1654), together with Schütz and Schein, the greatest German musician of the seventeenth century. Organist and conductor at Halle. (3) Portrait engraving from his *Tabulatura Nova* (see fig. 5). (4) Signature of a treatise of 22nd December 1624. Dresden, State archives of Saxony. (5) Title-page for the first part of Scheidt's principal work *Tabulatura Nova*, for the organ, Hamburg, 1624.

I   2   3

4   5

(**1**) Thomas Selle (1599–1663), director of church music at Itzehoe and at Hamburg. Engraving by D. Diercksen, 1653.
(**2**) Jan Adams Reinken (1623—1722), organist of the church of St. Katharine at Hamburg, was visited several times by
J. S. Bach, while the latter was at Lüneburg. Unsigned engraving. (**3**) Vincent Lübeck (1654–1740), organist at Stade
and at the church of St. Katharine at Hamburg. Pastel portrait in the museum of Altona. (**4**) Franz Tunder (1614–67)
was the predecessor of his son-in-law, Dietrich Buxtehude, as organist of the Marienkirche at Hamburg. Original
manuscript of the solo part of the soprano aria, *Ein kleines Kindelein*, with instrumental accompaniment. Lübeck,
State Library. (**5**) From J. A. Reinken's original manuscript of Sweelinck's *Theory and Instruction in Composition*,
1670. Hamburg, State and University Library.

(1) Johann Crüger (1598–1662), composer of hymns, organist of the church of St. Nicholas at Berlin. Engraving by G. P. Busch, 1713. (2) Johann Sebastiani (1622–82), court musician to the Prince of Brandenburg at Königsberg. Title-page to the Passion Music *The Life and Death of Jesus Christ*, Königsberg, 1672. (3) Jacob Kremberg (*c.* 1650–*c.* 1720). Engraved title-page to the collection of arias *Musikalische Gemütsergötzung* (*Musical Pleasures*), with accompaniment for lute, angelica, viola da gamba, or guitar, Dresden, 1689. Engraving by M. Bodenehr, after Sam. Bottschild.

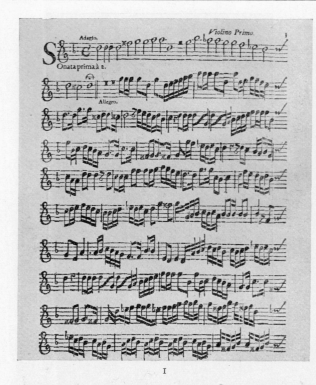

1

2

3

4

(1) Johann Rosenmüller (*c.* 1620–84), master of instrumental composition, latterly court musician at Wolfenbüttel. Page 1 of his last work, *Sonate a 2–5 stromenti da arco*, Nuremberg, 1682.   (2) Andreas Hammerschmidt (1612–75), composer of church music, a worthy contemporary of H. Schütz.   Organist at Zittau.   Engraving by S. Weiss, 1646. (3) Adam Krieger (1634–66), composer of vocal music (pupil of S. Scheidt) in Leipzig and Dresden.   Engraving by Chr. Rombstedt, after J. C. Höckner.   (4) Werner Fabricius (1633–79), organist at the church of St. Nicholas in Leipzig. Engraving by Ph. Kilian, after Sam. Bottschild, 1671.

1

2

3

4

5

(1) Sigmund Theophil (Gottlieb) Staden (1607–55), son of Johann Staden (see fig. 3, p. 165), organist of the church of St. Laurence at Nuremberg. Engraving by J. Sandrart, 1669, after M. Herr. (See also fig. 3, p. 181.) (2) Wolfgang Carl Briegel (1626–1712), court musician at Darmstadt. Engraving by E. Nessenthaler, after J. H. Leuchter, 1691. (3) Samuel Bockshorn (Capricornus: 1629–65), court musician at Stuttgart. Engraving by Ph. Kilian, 1659. (4) Engraved title-page to Funeral Songs (*Klag-, Trauer- und Valetgesänge*) (*Songs of Lament, Mourning, and Farewell*), by S. Th. Staden, Nuremberg, 1640. Engraving by P. Truschel. (5) Johann Caspar v. Kerll (1627–93), court musician at Munich (see p. 183). Engraving by C. G. Amling.

1

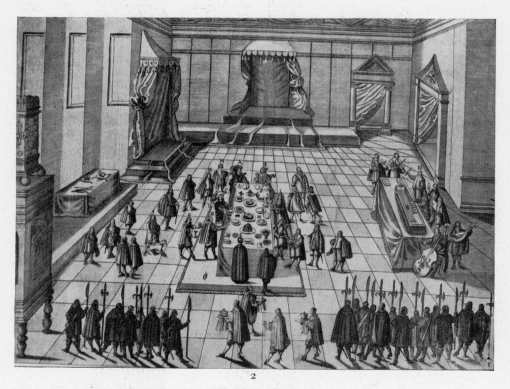

2

(1) 'Das Fried- und Freudenmahl' ('The Feast of Peace and Joy') to celebrate the end of the Thirty Years' War, in the town hall of Nuremberg, 25th September 1649. Four choirs took part in the concert at the banquet, and were conducted by Sigmund Staden (see fig. 1, p. 173). Engraving by Wolfgang Kilian. (2) Banquet on the occasion of the oath of fealty to the Emperor Ferdinand III (reigned 1637–57), in the Hofburg, Vienna, showing an orchestra of eight musicians. Unsigned engraving, dated 1652.

I

2

(1) 'The Concerto' (chitarrone or bass lute, two violins, guitar). Engraving by Etienne Picart, after the painting by Domenichino (Domenico Zampieri) in the Louvre, Paris. (2) A company of musicians. 'Chanson à 5 parties,' accompanied by lute and viola da gamba (basse de viole). Engraving 'L'ouie,' by Abraham Bosse.

I

2

(**1**) Gerard von Honthorst: 'The Musicians' (lute, violins, flageolet). Petersburg, Hermitage. Photograph by Hanfstaengl. (**2**) Gonzales Conques: 'The Duet' (lute, guitar). Brussels, Musée de Peinture. Photograph by the museum.

1

2

3

(1) Theodor Rombouts: Company engaged in music (guitar, lute). Munich, Old Pinakothek. Photograph by Hanf-staengl. (2) Jan Fyt: Group of instruments (guitar, violins, lute, dolcian, pochette-kit, or sordini) from a picture of still life. Vienna, Art History Museum. Photograph by Löwy. (3) Pieter Lastmann (Rembrandt's master): Group of singers and instrumentalists (violin, tambourine, trombone, bombard, bass viola da gamba, lute), from the painting 'King David in the Temple,' 1618. Brunswick Museum. Photograph by Bruckmann.

3

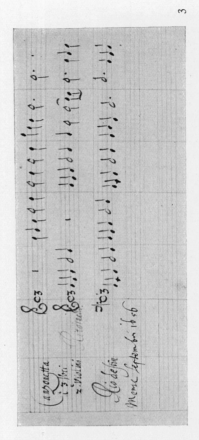

4

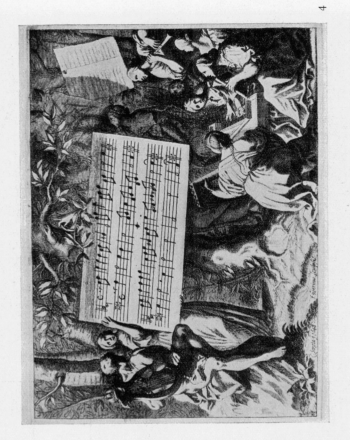

1

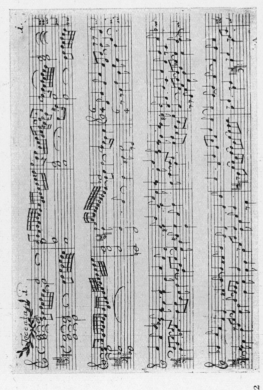

2

Johann Jacob Froberger (1616–67), the greatest German master of the clavier and organ before J. S. Bach. Pupil of Frescobaldi and organist of the imperial court of Vienna. (1) *Lament on the Death of King Ferdinand IV* from the *Libro quarto di Toccate, Ricercari, Caprici . . for organ or cembalo. Autograph copy dedicated to the Emperor Ferdinand III, 1656. Vienna, National Library. (2) Toccata I from the printed work *Partite di Toccate, Canzone, Ricercate. . . di Cimbali, Organi e Instromenti*, Mainz, 1603; Ludwig Bourgeat. (Froberger may be considered the originator of the Clavier Suite.) Wolfgang Ebner (1612–65), organist to the imperial court, and choir-master of St. Stephen's Church. Vienna, National Library. (3) Catalogue of the compositions of the Emperor Leopold I (reigned 1657–1705), compiled by Ebner, with the date of each composition in the emperor's hand. Vienna, National Library. (4) *Aria Imperatoris Ferdinandi III. XXXVI modis variata pro Cimbalo* (thirty-six variations for clavier on a theme by the Emperor Ferdinand III), Prague, 1648. Engraving by F. Henricus, after C. Screta. Only known copy in the National Library, Vienna.

2

4

3

1

3

(1) Christian Michel [Michaël?], organist of the church of St. Nicholas and St. Paul in Leipzig (c. 1645). Engraved title-page to book on tablature, *For the Clavier*, Brunswick, 1645. Only known copy is in the State Library, Berlin. (2) to (4) Johann Kuhnau (1660–1722). The originator of the clavier sonata with several movements; Bach's predecessor as cantor of the Thomas Schule, and as music director at the Leipzig University. (2) Engraved title-page of Johann Kuhnau's *Fresh Fruits for the Clavier (frischen Clavierfrüchten), or Seven Sonatas . . . for the Clavier*, Leipzig, 1696. (3) Engraved title-page of *Musical Representation of several Biblical Stories in Six Sonatas for the Clavier*, Leipzig, 1710. (Edition, with Italian title-page, of the Programme Sonatas (*The Fight between David and Goliath*), from the same work. (Music engraving.)

1

2

3

(1) Johann Jacob Walther (1650 until after 1700). Violinist at the courts of Saxony and of Mainz. Together with Biber, he was the most brilliant violin virtuoso of his time. Page 1 of the *Hortulus chelicus*, Mainz, 1688, L. Bourgeat. Title of the second edition, 1694: 'Richly blooming Garden of Pleasure for the violinist (Wohlgepflanzter violinischer Lustgarten), in which . . . the road to Perfection is made plain to all amateurs, also, by the occasional use of 2, 3, 4 strings at once, the most delightful harmony is produced.' (2) Heinrich Ignaz Franz Biber (1644–1704), Kapellmeister (director of music) to the Archbishop of Salzburg. Portrait from *Sonatae Violino solo*, Salsburg, 1681. Engraving by Paul Seel. (3) Johann Paul von Westhoff (1656–1705), director of chamber music to the court of Saxony, at Dresden. As violin virtuoso he travelled over half Europe; after A. Moser he is 'the greatest master of polyphonic music for the violin, prior to Bach.' Sheet D 4 (*Imitatione delle Campane*), from the six *Sonate a Violino solo con Basso continuo*, Dresden, 1694. Only known copy at Dresden, Landesbibliothek.

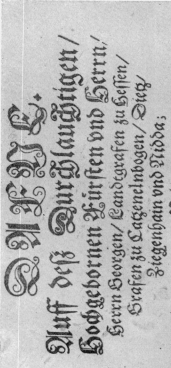

(1) Title-page to the libretto of the first German opera, *Daphne*, composed by Heinrich Schütz (Breslau, 1627), performed for the marriage of Princess Sophie Eleonore of Saxony and Landgrave George II of Hesse-Darmstadt, at the castle of Hartenfels, near Torgau. Nothing but the text of the libretto by Martin Opitz, which was derived from Rinuccini's libretto (see fig. 4, p. 154), remains in the National Library in Dresden. The score was probably destroyed by fire in 1760. (2) Group of musicians (in a grotto) from the so-called Stuttgart Rossballett (Equestrian Ballet): Processions and tournaments at the wedding celebrations of Duke Ludwig Friedrich of Württemberg, July 1617. No. 44 of the designs for panels drawn by Mattäus Merian. (3) Vignette ('The Muse of Song') from the fourth part of *Frauenzimmergesprächsspiele* (musical dialogues for female voices). George Philip Harsdörffer, Nuremberg, 1644. Contains the printed text, and the music composed by Sigmund Gottlieb Staden (see fig. 1, p. 173). *Seelewig* (sacred pastoral poem). Songs in the Italian style. The oldest German opera extant.

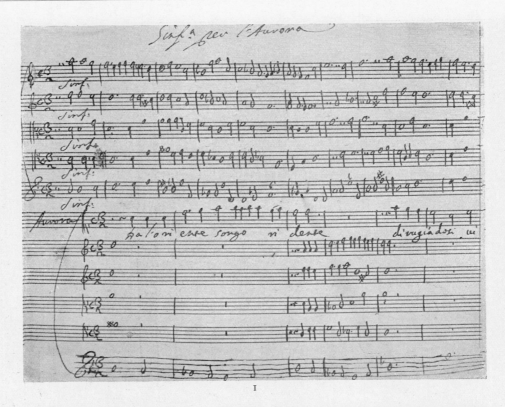

1

2

(**1**) Francesco Cavalli (Pier Francesco Caletti-Bruni, 1602–76). Organist and choir-master of the church of St. Mark in Venice; as operatic composer, a worthy successor of Monteverdi. Prologue to the opera (*Favola drammatica*) *L'Egisto*, Vienna, 1642. Libretto by Giovanni Faustini. Score in the composer's own hand. Vienna, National Library.
(**2**) Tournament scene from the opera *La Gara*, Vienna, 1652. Libretto by Alberto Vimina. Music by Antonio Bertali, director of music at the imperial court (1605–69). Scenario by Giovanni Burnacini.

I

2

3

Engravings of the scenarios for the operas (performed at Munich) by the Bavarian music director Johann Caspar v. Kerll (1627–93) (see fig. 5, p. 173).   (1) From the opera (*drama regio musicale*) *L'Erinto*, performed in 1661 and 1671. Libretto by Pietro Paolo Bissari.   (2) and (3) Two scenes from *La Fedra incoronata*, performed in 1662 on the occasion of the christening of the Electoral Prince Max Emanuel.   Libretto by P. P. Bissari.   Music probably by J. C. v. Kerll.

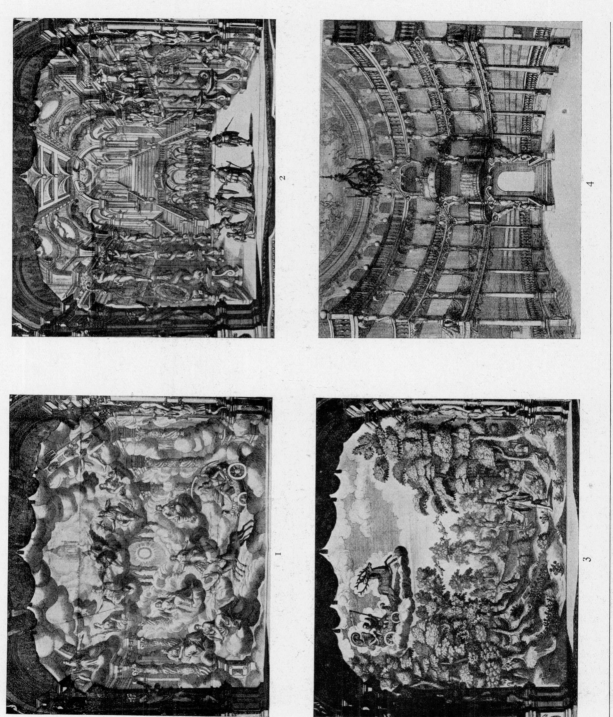

Engravings of scenarios for the opera *Servio Tullio*, Munich, 1685–6. Libretto by Ventura Terzago; music by his brother Agostino Steffani, afterwards director of chamber music and diplomatist (1654–1728); scenery by Domenico Mauro. (1) Prologue in heaven. (2) Hall in the king's palace. (3) Forest scene. (4) View of the boxes in the Hoftheater at Munich. Engravings by Michael Wening.

Interior view of the theatre, built of wood on the Cortina by the engineer Lodovico Burnacini, for the production of the opera *Il pomo d'oro* by W. A. Cesti (see fig. 1, p. 186), Vienna.   End of 1666 or beginning of 1667.   Etching by Franz Geffels.

1

2

Two representations of the festivities for the marriage of the Emperor Leopold I with the Infanta Margarethe of Spain. (Vienna, December 1666 and January 1667.)   (**1**) Scene representing Hell, from the opera (*festa teatrale*), *Il pomo d'oro*. Libretto by Francesco Sbarra; music by Marc' Antonio Cesti (1618–69) (cf. fig. 2, p. 159); scenery by Lodovico Burnacini. Etching by Matthias Küsel, from the libretto published in 1667–8.   (**2**) The so-called Rossballet (Equestrian Ballet), or *Festa a Cavallo* (Tournament), in the Hofburg at Vienna, 14th (? 24th) January 1667: *La contessa dell' aria e dell' acqua*. Libretto by Francesco Sbarra; music by Ant. Bertali (music for trumpets by Joh. Heinrich Schmelzer); scenery by Carlo Pasetti.   Etching from 'Festivals at the Marriage of Leopold I,' Vienna, 1667.

(1) and (2) Engraved title-pages to two libretti for operas by Lully: to the opera *Bellérophon* (1679), libretto by Thomas Corneille, and to the royal ballet, *Le triomphe de l'Amour* (1681), libretto by Benserade and Quinault. Engraving by Daniel Marot, after Jean Bérain. (3) Jean François Lallouette (1651–1728), violinist and composer, secretary to Lully. Engraving by J. Tardieu the Younger, after Ferdinand. (4) Michel Richard de Lalande (1657–1726), composer of motets, court director of music. Engraving by H. S. Thomassin, after J. B. Santerre.

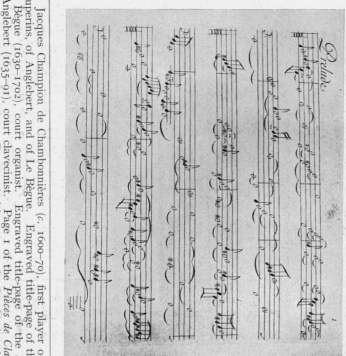

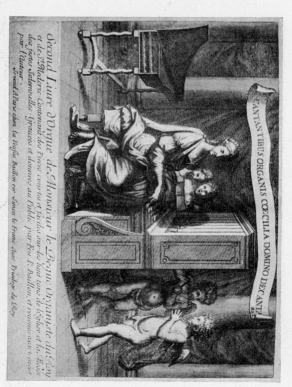

(1) Jacques Champion de Chambonnières (c. 1600–70), first player of the clavecin (harpsichord) at the court of Louis XIV. Teacher of the elder Couperins, of Anglebert, and of Le Bègue. Engraved title-page of the first book of *Pièces de Clavecin*, Paris, 1670. Engraving by Jollain. (2) Nicolas Le Bègue (1630–1702), court organist. Engraved title-page of the *Second livre d'orgue*, Paris, c. 1680. Engraving by P. Baillon. (3) Jean Henri d'Anglebert (1635–91), court clavecinist. Page 1 of the *Pièces de Clavecin . . . avec la manière de les jouer*, Paris, 1689. (4) Marin Marais (1656–1728) (see fig. 4, p. 193). Engraved title-page to the five books of *Pièces de Violes*, Paris, 1686–1725. Engraving by Trouvain, after Pezay.

(1) Matthew Locke (*c.* 1630–77), composer to Charles II, one of the most famous English musicians of the Restoration. Oil painting in the Music School, Oxford.   (2) 'Ayre' from a Suite for Wind Instruments 'for His Majestys Sagbutts and Cornetts,' composed by Locke for the coronation of Charles II.   Manuscript score.   Add. MSS. 1780.   London, British Museum.   (3) John Blow (1649–1708), composer of church music, organist of Westminster Abbey, and master to H. Purcell.   Engraving by Robert White (from Blow's *Amphion Anglicus*, London, 1700).   (4) Thomas Britton (1643/4–1714), coal merchant and lover of music ('the musical small-coal man').   One of the founders of the organization of concerts in London.   Portrait in oils by G. J. Wallaston (1703) in the National Portrait Gallery, London.

(**1**) Figurine for the masque composed by Thomas Campion (1567–1620), for the wedding of Lord James Hayes (Whitehall, 1607). The masque, forerunner of the opera, was much favoured in England at the beginning of the seventeenth century. (**2**) Henry Purcell (1658–95), composer to the king, England's greatest musician, the most important of the masters belonging to the brief flowering of English opera at the time of the Restoration. End of the *Fantasia upon one note* for five viols, in the composer's manuscript. Add. MSS. 30930. London, British Museum. (**3**) and (**4**) Portrait in oils of Henry Purcell, and of his younger brother, Daniel Purcell, the organist (*c.* 1660–1717), by John Closterman. London, National Portrait Gallery.

I   2   3

4

(1) Apostolo Zeno (1668–1750), the predecessor, as librettist, of Metastasio.   Copper-plate engraving by Andrea Zucchi,
after Friedrich Brancovich.   (2) Alessandro Scarlatti (1659–1725), the leader of the so-called Neapolitan school founded
by him and Francesco Provenzale in the late seventeenth century; this school took undisputed first rank in the field of
opera and dominated the period of *Bel canto*.   Portrait in oils in the Liceo Musicale, Bologna.   (3) Pietro Metastasio
(actually, Trapassi, 1698–1782), poet at the court of Vienna; the most famous and prolific writer of libretti of the eighteenth
century.   Copper-plate engraving by Paolo Caronni.   (4) Alessandro Scarlatti: quartet from the third act of the opera
Telemaco (text by Carlo Sigismund Capeci, Rome, 1718).   (Note in libretto: 'Questa e la centesima nona opera teatrale
da lui composta.')   From the manuscript score at Vienna, National Library.

(1) Niccolo Jommelli (1714–74), from 1753–69 court musician at Stuttgart; known, in his capacity as composer of operas, as the 'Italian Gluck.'   Portrait in oils in the Liceo Musicale, Bologna.   (2) Tommaso Traetta (1727–79), composer to the court of Empress Catherine II. Portrait in oils at Naples, Conservatorio San Pietro a Majella.   (3) Francesco Feo (c. 1785 to after 1745), in later life director of the Conservatorio della Pietà at Naples.   Portrait in oils in the Liceo Musicale, Bologna. (4) Niccolo Porpora (1686–1767), c. 1750 co-music director with Hasse at Dresden, later director of the Conservatorio di Sant' Onofrio in his native town of Naples. Copper-plate engraving by G. Magnio.   (5) Giovanni Battista Pergolesi (1710–36), composer of the intermezzo *La serva padrona* (1733), the prototype of the Italian *opéra bouffe* and the French *opéra comique* of the eighteenth century. Silhouette engraving after the medallion by T. Mercandetti (1806).
    (6) Leonardo Leo (1694–1744), master of Jommelli and Piccinni. Portrait in oils in the Liceo Musicale, Bologna.

Salà del Palazzo Reale apparata per la Serenata

(1) Performance of the dramatic cantata (*festa teatrata*) *La contesa de' numi*, composed by Leonardo Vinci (1690–1732) on the occasion of the birth of the Dauphin, with libretto by Pietro Metastasio; the performance took place on 27th November 1729 in the palace of Cardinal Melchior de Polignac at Rome. Painting by Giovanni Paolo Panini. Paris, Louvre. Photograph by the museum. (2) Performance in the Royal Palace (Naples, 6th November 1747) of the Serenata *Il sogno di Olimpia* by Giuseppi di Majo (1698–1772); libretto by Gluck's librettist Raniero di Calsabigi. Copper-plate engraving by Giuseppe Vasi, after Vincenzo Rè.

1

2

3

4

5

(1) Nicola Piccini (1728–1800), Gluck's rival in Paris; one of the most prolific composers of opera.   Copper-plate en-
graving by H. Panquet, after Bergeret.   (2) Antonio Sacchini (1734–86), composer of the opera *Oedipe à Colone*, in which
Gluck's influence is apparent.   Copper-plate engraving by Augustin de Saint-Aubin (1786), after C. N. Cochin the
Younger (1782).   (3) Domenico Cimarosa (1749–1801), composer of the *opéra bouffe, Il matrimonio segreto* (Vienna, 1792).
Copper-plate engraving by Giuseppe Asioli (1816), after E. Vigée-Le Brun.   (4) Francesco di Majo (*c.* 1740–70), organist
at the Royal Chapel, Naples, and composer of operas.   Portrait in oils in the Liceo Musicale, Bologna.   (5) Giovanni
Paesiello (1740–1816), court musician at Naples; composer of the *opéra bouffe, La molinara* (Naples, 1788).   Copper-plate
engraving by E. Beisson of a drawing by Lefort, after the picture by E. Vigée-Le Brun.   Paris, Louvre.

3

1

2

4

(1) Antonio Caldara (1670–1736), vice-music director at the imperial court of Vienna; composer of operas and of church and instrumental music. Portrait in oils in the Liceo Musicale, Bologna. (2) Scenario from the *dramma per musica* (Pasticcio) *Giunio Bruto overo La caduta de Tarquini*. Music by Carlo Francesco Cesarini (Act I), Antonio Caldara (Act II), and Alessandro Scarlatti (Act III). Viennese presentation score (Rome, 1707), with water-colours by Filippo Juvara. Vienna, National Library. (3) Attilio Ariosti (1666 – *c.* 1740), diplomatist and composer to the court of Queen Sophy Charlotte of Prussia. Copper-plate engraving by C. Grignion (1776). (4) Giuseppe Gazzaniga (1743–1818), music director at Crema Cathedral; composer of operas and church music. Portrait in oils in the Liceo Musicale, Bologna.

(1) Francesco Bianchi (1752–1810), composer of operas, and conductor in London and Dublin. Engraving by A. R. Burt (London, 1805), after a drawing by G. Chinnery. (2) Vincenzo Righini (1756–1812), composer of operas; after 1793 director of music at the Royal Opera House, Berlin. Stippled engraving by F. W. Bollinger, Berlin, 1803. (3) Antonio Salieri (1750–1825), composer of operas (*Les Danaides*, Paris, 1784), musician to the imperial court of Vienna, teacher of Beethoven and Schubert. Lithograph by Fr. Rehberg, Vienna, 1821. Operatic singers: (4) Francesca Cuzzoni-Sandoni (1700–70) and her rival Faustina Hasse-Bordoni (1700–81). (5) Francesco Bernardi detto il Senesino (1680–?) and Carlo Broschi-Farinelli (1705–82), the two most popular sopranos (castrate) of their time. Unsigned English copper-plate engraving. (6) Giovanni Carestina detto Cusanio (*c.* 1705–*c.* 1760). Mezzotint engraving by J. Faber (London, 1735), after G. Knapton. (7) Felice Salimbeni (*c.* 1712–51). Drawing by G. Fr. Schmidt, Berlin, 1751. (8) Liugi Marchesi (Marchesini, 1755–1829). Stippled engraving by L. Schiavonetti (London, 1790), after R. Conway.

(**1**) Angelo Maria Monticelli (*c.* 1715–64).   Mezzotint engraving by J. Faber, after Andrea Casali.   (**2**) Carlo Broschi-Farinelli (1705–82) (see fig. 5, p. 206).   Oil painting in the Liceo Musicale, Bologna.   (**3**) Domenico Annibali (*c.* 1750). Pastel by Anton Raphael Mengs (1745) in the Dresden Art Gallery.   Photograph by the museum.   (**4**) The singer Anna Zamperini as Cecchina in Piccinni's most successful *opéra bouffe, La buona figliuola*.   Mezzotint engraving by J. Finlayson (London, 1769), after N. Hone.

(1) Giac. Ant. Perti (1661–1756). (2) Giacomo Predieri the Younger (d. 1753). (3) Marc' Ant. Bononcini (c. 1670–1726).
(4) Giovanni Battista Bononcini (c. 1665–c. 1739). (5) Francesco Durante (1684–1755). (6) Domenico Scarlatti (1685–1757).
(7) Benedetto Marcello (1686–1739). (8) Francesco Antonio Vallotti (1697–1780). (9) Giovanni Battista Sammartini
(1701–75), Gluck's master. Figs. 1–5 and 9, after oil paintings in the Liceo Musicale, Bologna.

(1) Francesco Durante (see fig. 5, p. 208): Magnificat in E flat major (for four voices with instrumental accompaniment). Manuscript score. Berlin, National Library. (2) Padre Giambattista Martini (1706–84), famous scientific musician, teacher and composer of Bologna. Engraving (by Francesco Rosaspina), after the oil painting in the Liceo Musicale, Bologna. (3) Luigi Boccherini (1743–1805), instrumental composer and violoncello virtuoso. Unsigned stippled engraving, after Lefevre. (4) Francesco Fortunati (1746–c. 1815), composer and court musician at Parma. Portrait in oils in the Liceo Musicale, Bologna. (5) Muzio Clementi (c. 1750–1832), piano virtuoso, teacher, and composer. Stippled engraving by Thomas Hardy, London, 1794.

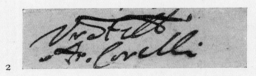

Arcangelo Corelli (1653–1713), director of music to Cardinal Pietro Ottoboni, Rome, founder of the so-called Roman school of violin playing, the greatest composer of classical Italian violin music, and creator of the 'Concerto Grosso.' (**1**) Engraving by van der Gucht, after the portrait by the English artist Hugh Howard, painted in 1700. (**2**) Signature of a letter to his brother Ippolito, Rome, 1705. Formerly in Cologne, Heyer Museum. (**3**) Title-page to the *Trio Sonatas*, Op. 1, Rome, 1681. (**4**) Engraved title-page to the *Trio Sonatas*, Op. 3, Rome, 1689. Engraving by Nicol Dorigny. (**5**) Engraved title-page to the *Concerti grossi*, Op. 6, Amsterdam (*c.* 1715), Etienne Roger. Engraving by G. van der Gouwen, after Francesco Trevisani.

(1) Francesco Geminiani (1674–1762), from 1714 onwards was active in London as violin virtuoso and composer, a pupil of Corelli and Scarlatti; author of the first genuine Violin Method, 1731. Mezzotint by James MacArdell, after Thomas Jenkins. (2) Tommaso Vitali detto Vitalino (c. 1670–1745), director of music to the Duke of Modena; as composer he is remembered chiefly for his *Ciaccona*. Portrait in oils in the Liceo Musicale, Bologna. (3) Antonio Vivaldi (c. 1680–1743), director of the Conservatorium Ospedale della Pietà in Venice. The greatest master of the violin concerto and the most eminent Italian instrumental composer in the age of Joh. Seb. Bach. Engraving by F. M. la Cave, 1725(?). (4) Engraved title-page to *Trio Sonatas*, Op. 1, by Antonio Veracini, Florentine composer of chamber music, Florence, 1692. Etching by F. Aquila.

(1) Giuseppe Tartini (1692–1770), violin virtuoso and composer, founder of the school of violin playing at Padua (1728) and discoverer of artificial harmonics. Portrait in oils in the Liceo Musicale, Bologna. (2) Signature of a letter from Tartini to Padre Martini in Bologna, Padua, 1741. Formerly in Cologne, Heyer Museum. (3) Title-page to twelve *Violin Sonatas* by Felice Giardini, violin virtuoso (1716–96), after 1750 in London (London, 1765). Engraving by Fr. Bartolozzi, after G. B. Cipriani. (4) Pietro Locatelli (1693–1764), violinist and composer, a worthy pupil of Corelli. Engraving by Lambert, after a drawing in the possession of J. B. Cartiers. (5) Antonio Lolli (c. 1730–1802), virtuoso, a forerunner of Paganini. Drawing by Hardrich. Berlin, Staatsbibliothek. (6) Pietro Nardini (1722–93), pupil of Tartini, court musician in Florence. Engraving by G. B. Cecchi, after M. Vestri.

(1) Gaetano Pugnani (1731–89), director of music, and from 1770 conductor at the Hoftheater, Turin; teacher of Viotti. Portrait in oils in Liceo Musicale, Bologna (see also fig. 1, p. 266). (2) Nicolo Mestrino (1748–89), violinist and conductor, settled latterly in Paris. Engraving by Lambert, after a drawing in the possession of J. B. Cartiers. (3) Giov. Battista Viotti (1753–1824), the 'Father of Modern Violin Technique,' and one of the most eminent composers for his instrument. Miniature by Trossarelli. Paris, Musée de l'Opéra. (4) Title-page to the Paris edition of Viotti's *Six Violin Duets*, Op. 5.

1

2

3

4

5

(1) André Cardinal Destouches (1662–1749), operatic composer favoured by Louis XIV; court musician after 1728.   Pastel portrait, attributed to Quentin de la Tour.   (2) Engraved title-page to Destouches' opera *Marthésie, première reine des Amazones* (libretto by de la Mothe; Fontainebleau and Paris, 1699), Paris, 1700.   Engraving by P. Giffart, after J. Bérain.   (3) André Campra (1660–1744), the most eminent French operatic composer of the period between Lully and Rameau.   Engraving by Gérard Edelinck, after André Bouys.   (4) Jean Philippe Rameau (1683–1764), the greatest master of French opera of the eighteenth century, and founder of the modern system of harmony.   Engraving by L. C. de Carmontelle.   (5) Rameau.   Engraving by Benoist after J. Restout (the bust by J. J. Caffieri).

I

2

3

(**1**) Jean Philippe Rameau (1683–1764): *La Dauphine* (piece for the clavier composed in 1745 for the marriage of the Dauphine to Princess Maria Josepha of Saxony, not included in Rameau's *Livres de Clavecin*. Manuscript. Paris, Bibliothèque nationale. (**2**) Etienne Nicolas Méhul (1763–1817), composer of the opera *Joseph* (*Joseph in Egypt*, Paris, 1807). Portrait in oils by Joseph Ducreux in the museum, Versailles. (**3**) François Joseph Gossec (1734–1829), composer of operas and oratorios, etc. Aquatint by Edme Quenedey, 1813.

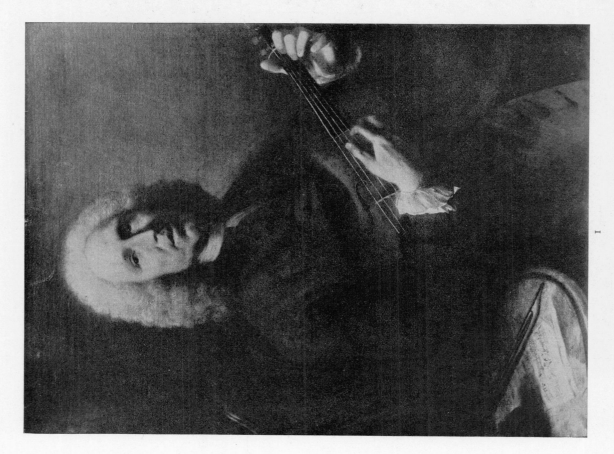

(1) Jean Philippe Rameau (1683–1764). Portrait in oils by J. B. S. Chardin in the Dijon Museum. Photograph by the museum. (2) Performance of Voltaire's comédie-ballet *La Princesse de Navarre*, with music by J. P. Rameau, on the occasion of the marriage at Versailles of the Dauphin to Princess Maria Josepha of Saxony, 23rd February 1745. Drawing by C. N. Cochin the Younger (sketch for the engraving), in the Louvre, Paris.

(1) Charles Simon Favart (1710–92), dramatic poet, one of the originators of the French operetta. Copper-plate engraving by C. A. Littret, after J. E. Liotard. (2) André Danican Philidor (1726–95), composer of operas and noted chess player. Copper-plate engraving by A. de Saint-Aubin (1772), after C. N. Cochin the Younger. (3) Pierre Alexandre Monsigny (1729–1817), one of the most important figures in French comic opera. Oil painting by Thévenin, Paris, Musée de l'Opéra. (4) André Erneste Modeste Grétry (1742–1813), the leading composer of opéra comique. Oil painting by Elizabeth Vigée-Le Brun. Versailles Museum. (5) Nicolas d'Alayrac (1753–1809), composer of operettas. Aquatint by Edme Quenedey, 1809. (6) Nicolo Isouard (Nicolo da Malta, 1775–1818), Boïldieu's rival as a composer of operas. Unsigned drawing. Paris, André Tessier Collection.

1

2

3

4

5

6

(1) Marthe Rochois (1650–1728), singer in grand opera at Paris under Lully. Copper-plate engraving (Paris, I. Mariette).
(2) Pierre Jeliote (Jeliotte, 1711–82). Copper-plate engraving by A. de Saint-Aubin (1771), after Cochin the Younger 1767. (3) Joseph le Gros (1739–93), Gluck's favourite tenor and leader of the *concerts spirituels*. Copper-plate engraving by Marot, after Le Clerc. (4) Marie Justine Favart, *née* Duronceray (1727–72), actress and singer, wife of the dramatic poet C. S. Favart. Copper-plate engraving by J. J. Flipart (1762), after C. Cochin the Younger (1753).
(5) Antoinette Cécile Saint-Huberty, *née* Clavel (1756–1812), an opera singer of whom Gluck had a high opinion. Stippled engraving on copper by Endner, after Le Moine. (6) Joseph Caillot (1732–1816), actor and singer in the Italian comedy at Paris. Copper-plate engraving by S. C. Miger, after G. Voiriot,

I

2

3

(1) 'Le concert champêtre': Transverse flute, viola da gamba, theorbo, and singers.   Engraving on copper by Benoit Audran, after Antoine Watteau.   (2) Jean de Julienne as a performer on the viola da gamba (bass viol), and the painter Watteau.   Engraving on copper by N. H. Tardieu (1674–1749).   (3) 'L'assemblée au concert.'   Engraving on copper by F. Dequevauviller, after N. Lavreince (c. 1785).

1

2

3   4   5

(1) Jean Ferry Rebel (1661–1747), one of the first French composers of chamber music. Drawing by Antoine Watteau from the David Weill Collection. (2) Louis Nicolas Clérambault (1676–1749), court organist, composer of cantatas. Engraving on copper by L'Empereur. (3) Nicolas Bernier (1664–1734), music director of Sainte Chapelle, Paris; composer of cantatas. Engraving on copper by E. Ficquet, after L. N. (4) Louis Marchand (1669–1732), organist at the Royal Chapel, composer for the organ and clavier. Engraving on copper by C. Dupuis, after Robert. (5) Louis Claude Daquin (1694–1772), organist at the Royal Chapel, composer for the clavier. Engraving on copper by Petit, after C. Descombes, 1747.

(**1**) Armand Louis Couperin (1725–89), organist to the court; the leading French organist of his time.   Drawing by
Chrétien.   (**2**) Jean Baptiste Antoine Forqueray (1700–82), viola da gamba virtuoso.   Oil painting by J. M. Frédou, 1737.
(**3**) Jean Marie Leclair (1697–1764), violinist and composer for the violin.   Engraving by J. C. François, after a drawing
by Alexis Loir.   (**4**) Jean Pierre Guignon (Giovanni Pietro Ghignone, 1702–74), the last 'Roi des Ménétriers' (King of
Fiddlers); composer of chamber music.   Engraving on copper by Pinssio, after van Loo.   (**5**) Jean Jacques Beauvarlet,
called Charpentier (1730–64), organist and composer for the organ.   Engraving on copper by S. C. Miger, after C. N. Cochin
the Younger, 1781.   (**6**) Louis Joseph Francoeur (1738–1804), violinist and composer.   Engraving on copper by Mme
Lingée, after J. M. Moreau the Younger.   (**7**) The composer Michel de la Barre (c. 1675–1743/44), conducting a flute
concerto.   Contemporary French painting in the National Gallery, London.   (**8**) Pierre Gaviniés (1728–1800), violin
virtuoso, on whom Viotti conferred the title of the 'French Tartini.'   Drawing by Chrétien, after P. Guérin.

I

2   3

(1) Louis de Caix d'Hervelois (c. 1690–c. 1760), viola da gamba virtuoso and composer. Page 8 from Book I of *Pièces de Viole*, Paris, 1725 (French music copper-plate engraving). (2) Jean Joseph Cassanéa de Mondonville (1711–72), violin virtuoso and composer. Court musical director. Title-page to *Pièces de Clavecin avec voix ou violon*, Op. 5, Paris (c. 1748). Copper-plate engraving by Rue and M. Aubert, after F. Baillieul (script) and Rigaud (picture). (3) Portrait of Mondonville. Pastel by Quentin de la Tour. St. Quentin, Musée Lécuyer.

1

2

3

4

5

(1) Jean Benjamin de la Borde (1734–94), composer and writer on music. Etching by J. M. Moreau the Younger (1771), after Denon (1770). (2) Nicolas Séjan (1745–1819), court organist and composer. Copper-plate engraving by Mme Lingée, after C. N. Cochin the Younger (1780). (3) Jean d'Alembert le Rond (1717–83), philosopher and authority on acoustics; collaborator with Denis Diderot in the production of the *Encyclopédie méthodique*. Copper-plate engraving by Dupin the Younger, after A. Pujos (1774). (4) Jean Jacques Rousseau (1712–78), philosopher, composer (*Le devin du village*, 1752), and writer on music. Pastel by Quentin de la Tour. St. Quentin, Musée Lécuyer. Photograph by Bulloz. (5) François Devinne (1759–1803), flute virtuoso and composer. Oil painting by Louis David in the Museum, Brussels. Photograph by the museum.

(1) Antoine Watteau: 'Le Mézetin' (guitar). Petersburg, Hermitage. Photograph by Bruckmann.   (2) Nicolas Lancret: 'The Music Lesson' (angelica). Paris, Louvre. Photograph by Alinari.   (3) Jean Honoré Fragonard: 'La Gimard' (guitar). Paris, E. Rothschild Collection. Photograph by Braun, Clement & Co.   (4) Antoine Watteau: 'The Savoyard' (oboe). Petersburg, Hermitage. Photograph by Stoedtner.

1

2

(1) Pietro Longhi: Family concert (Milanese mandolines). Milan, Pinacoteca di Brera. Photograph by Alinari.
(2) Francesco Guardi: Concert in a Venetian institution for ladies. Munich, Old Pinakothek. Photograph by Bruckmann.

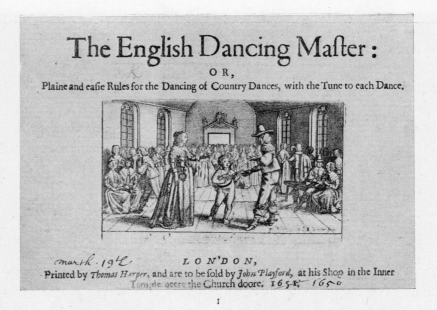

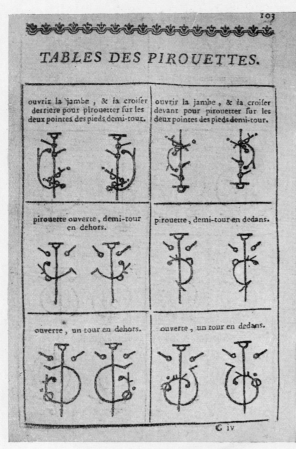

(1) Title-page to *The English Dancing Master*, London, 1657.   With etched vignette by Wenzel Hollar.   (2) 'Tables des Pirouettes,' from *Choréographie, ou l'art d'écrire la Dance par caractéres, figures et signes* by R. A. Feuillet, Paris, 1701. (3) Jean Georges Noverre (1727–1810), ballet master of the Grand Opera at Paris, who introduced reforms into dramatic ballet and was the author of *Lettres sur la danse et les ballets* (1760 and 1803).   Copper-plate engraving by B. Roger, after P. N. Guérin.

I

2

(1) Nicolas Lancret: The dancer Camargo.   Painting in the Museum at Nantes.   Photograph by Les Archives Photo-graphiques.   (2) 'Le bal paré.'   Etching by Antoine Jean Duclos, after a drawing by his master Augustin de Saint-Aubin.

1

2

3

4

5

(1) Thomas Augustine Arne (1710–78), composer of operas, the writer of the air of *Rule, Britannia*. Etching (caricature) by Fr. Bartolozzi. (2) John Christopher Pepusch (1667–1752), a versatile composer who set the *Beggar's Opera* to music (see fig. 2, p. 229). Unsigned oil painting. London, National Portrait Gallery. (3) William Shield (1748–1829), composer of operas and director of music at Covent Garden Theatre, London. Engraving by William Daniell (1809), after George Dance (1798). (4) Henry Carey (c. 1690–1743), composer of ballads and ballad operas. Copper-plate engraving by C. Grignion, after J. Worsdale. (5) Samuel Arnold (1740–1802), organist and composer of operas. Editor of Handel's works. Stippled engraving on copper by Ridley (1813), after J. Arnold.

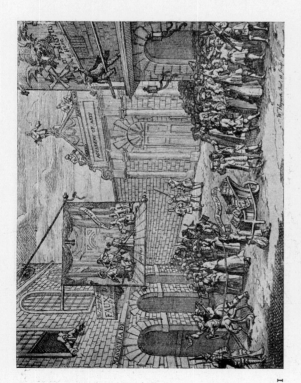

Descriptive pictures: (1) 'Masquerades and Operas.' Etching by William Hogarth (1724; second state, 1742). Satire on the success of Heidegger's masquerades and the idolizing of opera-singers. (2) 'The *Beggar's Opera* Burlesqued.' Etching by William Hogarth, 1728. Satire on the enormous success of the English *Beggar's Opera*, holding London society and Italian opera up to ridicule. (3) The Trial Scene (Act iii, sc. 11) from the *Beggar's Opera* by John Gay and J. C. Pepusch, London, 1728. Copper-plate engraving by William Blake, after William Hogarth. (4) 'A Sunday Concert.' Unsigned etching. Satire on London virtuosos of the late eighteenth century.

(**1**) John Banister the Younger (*c.* 1663–1735), violinist and composer. Mezzotint by John Smith, after T. Murray.
(**2**) William Boyce (1710–79), organist, composer to the king's orchestra and editor of the collection, *Cathedral Music.*
Portrait in oils by Thomas Hudson in the Music School, Oxford.   (**3**) John Hawkins (1719–89), author of *General History
of the Science and Practice of Music*, London, 1776.   Stippled engraving on copper by R. Clamp, after Harding and
J. Roberts.   (**4**) Charles Burney (1726–1814), author of *General History of Music*, London, 1776–89.   Drawing by George
Dance 1794.   London, National Portrait Gallery.

(1) 'The Music Lesson.'   Drawing in red chalk by Thomas Gainsborough.   London, British Museum.   (2) Caricature of the viola da gamba virtuoso C. F. Abel (1725–87).   Etching by W. N. Gardiner, 1787.   (3) The singer and lutanist Arabella Hunt (d. 1705).   Mezzotint by John Smith (1706), after G. Kneller.   (4) The infant prodigy Benjamin Hallet as violoncellist, 1749.   Mezzotint by J. MacArdell, after T. Jenkins.

(1) Unfretted clavichord in Louis XV style by Christian Gottlob Hubert, Ansbach (c. 1775).   (2) Spinet shaped like a small piano by Johann Heinrich Silbermann, Strasburg (c. 1770).   (3) Fretted clavichord by Johann Jacob Donat, Leipzig, 1700. All at Leipzig, Heyer Collection.

I

2

(1) 'Clavecin brisé' ('Clavecin de voyage'), by Jean Marius, Paris, 1713. A clavier which, for the purpose of travelling, could be separated into three parts (royal privilege of 18th September 1700). Frederick the Great is said to have taken a clavecin of this kind on his campaigns. Leipzig, Heyer Collection. (2) Two manual clavicembalo by Johann Heinrich Gräbner, Dresden, 1774. (As regards tone, one of the finest of the eighteenth-century clavecins still in existence.) Leipzig, Heyer Collection.

(1) Spinet by Joseph Mahoon, London (*c.* 1740). London, Victoria and Albert Museum. (2) Square piano (English table pianoforte) by John Broadwood, London, 1774. London, Collection of Messrs. John Broadwood & Sons. (3) Harpsichord with two manuals by Burkat Shudi (correctly: Burkhurdt Tschudi) (1702–73), London, 1771, made for his daughter Barbara, wife of his successor, John Broadwood. London, Broadwood Collection.

(1) Pianoforte ('Gravicimbalo col piano e forte') by the inventor Bartolomeo Cristofori, Florence, 1726.   Leipzig, Heyer
Collection (from the former collection of Alessandro Kraus, Florence).   The invention of the hammer action about 1709
by the clavier maker Cristofori, a native of Padua (1655–1731), was an event of overwhelming importance.   During
the second half of the eighteenth century it gradually superseded the old-fashioned makers of clavier, clavichord, and
cembalo.   (2) Pianoforte by Gottfried Silbermann, Freiberg (c. 1745), in the castle of Charlottenburg (cf. fig. 2, p. 267).
Cristofori's invention was established in Germany by the celebrated organ and clavier maker Silbermann, and spread
from there into England and France.   Photograph by the Staatliche Bildstelle, Berlin.

(1) Louis Michel van Loo: 'The Piano Concerto.' Petersburg, Hermitage. Photograph by Hanfstaengl. (2) Johann Nicolaus Grooth: Chamber music at the Bavarian court, with Prince Maximilian Joseph III (reigned 1745–77), who was a noted composer, playing the violoncello. Painting dated 1758. Munich, Residenzmuseum. Photograph by Dr. P. Wolff, Frankfort.

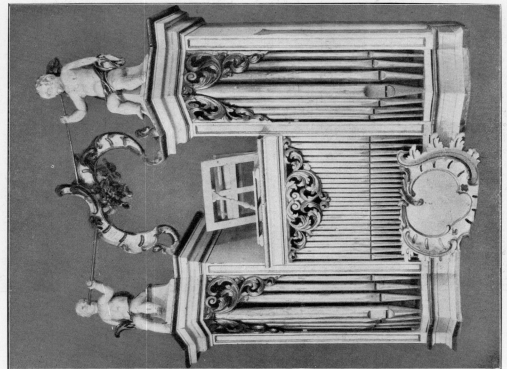

(1) Organ by Gottfried Silbermann, Freiburg (cf. fig. 2, p. 235), built 1723-4 for the Protestant church of Hilbersdorf, near Freiberg. Leipzig, Heyer Collection. (The only Silbermann organ owned by a museum.). (2) Dutch positive organ (c. 1750-70). From the former monastery of Schledenhorst, near Haldern, in the Rhine country. Leipzig, Heyer Collection. (English chamber organ of 1786; see fig. 1, p. 264.)

(1) 'Concert méchanique,' an automatic instrument invented by R. Richard, Paris, 1769. Engraving by de Longueil, after Ch. Eisen. (2) Johann Schenk, the viola da gamba virtuoso of Düsseldorf and Amsterdam. Mezzotint by his brother Peter Schenk (1645–1715). (3) Mme Henriette de France (daughter of King Louis XV) playing the viola da gamba. Painting by Jean Marc Nattier (1754), in the Palace, Versailles. (4) Man playing the viola d'amore. Unsigned. Engraving, early eighteenth century.

1

2

3

4

5

(**1**) 'Dame de qualité jouant de la guitarre' ('Lady of Quality playing the Guitar').   Engraving by A. Trouvain, Paris, 1694.
(**2**) The lutanist Adam Falkenhagen (1697–*c.* 1765) playing the theorbo.   Engraving by J. W. Stör, Nuremberg, 1758(?).
(**3**) Company engaged in music, 'Concerted piece for tympanum, lute, and German flute.'   Engraving by I. Danckerts.
(**4**) Woman harpist.   Engraving ('L'accord parfait': 'Perfect Harmony') by I. St. Helman (1777), after J. M. Moreau
    the Younger.   (**5**) Woman harpist.   English colour engraving by William Bond, after J. Russell.

(**1**) Copper-plate engraving representing various instruments ('Academia Musicale') from the educational work *Reglas y advertencias . . . de tañer todos los instrumentos*, by Pablo Minguet, Madrid, 1752–4.   (**2**) Theorbo by Johann Christian Hoffmann, instrument and lute maker to the court, a friend of Joh. Seb. Bach, Leipzig, 1720. Leipzig, Heyer Collection. (**3**) Guitar by Gioacchino Trotto, 1792. Leipzig, Heyer Collection.   (**4**) Neapolitan mandoline by Vincento Vinaccia, Naples, 1774. Berlin-Halensee, Wildhagen Collection.   (**5**) Theorbo by Sebastian Schelle, Nuremberg, 1774. Nuremberg, Germanic Museum.

The Hamburg craftsman, Joachim Tielke (1641–1719), stands out as the most prominent maker of lutes and violins in northern Germany. (1) to (5) Groups of instruments (showing fronts and backs) from the Heyer Collection at Leipzig: (1) Tenor viola da gamba, 1699; (2) Cithern, 1694; (3) Lute, 1676; (4) Descant viol, 1690; (5) Tenor viola da gamba, 1699. (6) Tenor viola da gamba, 1689, from the Hamburg Museum für Kunst und Gewerbe. (7) and (8) Cithern and guitar from the Victoria and Albert Museum, London. (9) Tenor viola da gamba (formerly attributed to Carlo Bergonzi, the pupil of Stradivarius) from the Heyer Collection, Leipzig.

I

4   2   3   5

(1) Viola d'amore (Liebesgeige) by Jacob Stainer (cf. fig. 3, p. 144), Absam, near Innsbruck, 1661, from the Salzburg Museum. Pencil drawing by Adolph Menzel, 1887, in the Berlin National Gallery.   (2) English viola d'amore of the oldest type. End of the seventeenth century, from the Victoria and Albert Museum, London.   (3) Pardessus de viole, five-stringed descant viol by Colin (or Collin), from Mirecourt, second half of the eighteenth century.   From the Wildhagen Collection, Berlin, Halensee.   (4) English viol (Liebesgeige, with seven playing strings and fourteen sympathetic or aliquot strings) by Johann Ulrich Eberle, Prague, 1739, from the Wildhagen Collection in Halensee, Berlin.   (5) Baryton (viola di bardone, the bass instrument of the viola d'amore) by Jacques Saintpre (Saint-Preux?), Berlin, seventeenth century.   Probably from the collection of J. J. Quantz.   From the Victoria and Albert Museum, London.

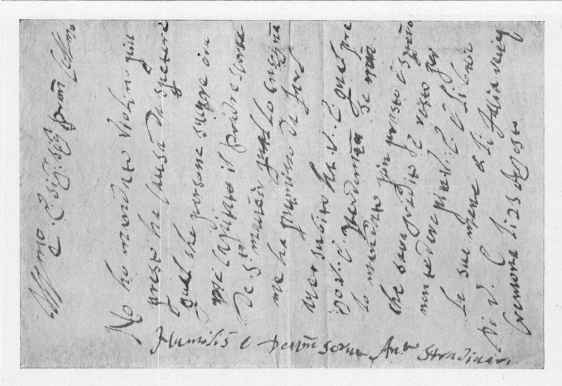

The art of violin-making associated with the name of Cremona reached its zenith in the greatest of all craftsmen in this field, the incomparable Antonio Stradivarius. (1) to (3) Violoncello of 1690, viola of 1690, violin of 1716, three instruments made for the Medici family. From the Museo del R. Instituto L. Cherubini, Florence (photograph by Brogi). (4) Autograph letter concerning the delivery of a violin, dated Cremona, 23rd August, c. 1715. The second of the only two Stradivarius letters as yet found. Formerly at the Heyer Museum, Cologne, now Mannheim, Dr. F. Reuther. From the Carlo Lozzi Collection, Rome.

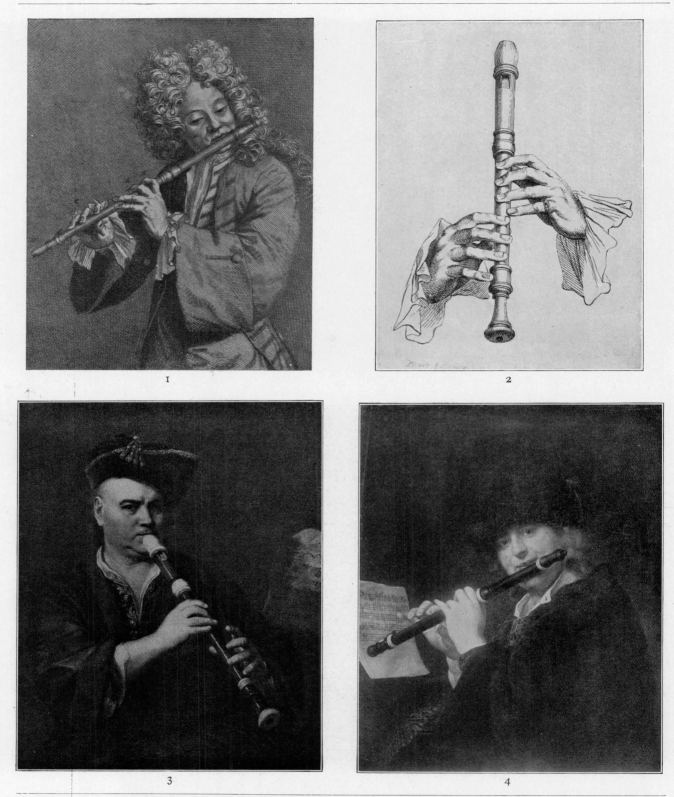

(**1**) Jacques (not Louis) Hotteterre le Romain (d. *c.* 1760), flute player to the king under Louis XIV and Louis XV. Engraving by Bernard Picart from Hotteterre's *Principes de la flute . . . et du hautbois*, Paris, 1707.   (**2**) Method of holding the flute-à-bec or flute douce.   Etching by B. Picart, from the same work.   (**3**) Janos Kupetzky (1667–1740): 'Der Blockflötenblaser' ('The Player on the Flute-à-bec') (self-portrait?), from the Museum der bildenden Künste, Budapest.   Photograph by Hanfstaengl.   (**4**) Janos Kupetzky: 'The Player of the German Flute' (*c.* 1730).   From the Germanic Museum, Nuremberg.   Photograph by Christof Müller, Nuremberg.

Georg Philipp Telemann (1681–1767), municipal director of music at Hamburg from 1721, was the most considerable German composer of the century, next to Handel and Bach, and was in his day far better known and more esteemed than the creator of the *Matthew Passion*. (**1**) Daniel Eberlin (*c. 1630–92*), composer and conductor, first of Telemann's fathers-in-law. Etching by Strauch, from Eberlin's *Violin Trios*, Nuremberg, 1675. (**2**) Portrait of Telemann. Mezzo-tint by V. D. Preisler, Nuremberg, 1750, after Ludwig Michael Schneider. (**3**) Page 1 of the *Tafelmusik* (*Musique de table partagée en 3 productions . . . à 7 instruments*), Hamburg, 1733. (**4**) Page 1 of the instrumental compositions (overtures, sinfonias, divertimenti, etc.), composed in his eighty-sixth year (1766) for the landgrave Ludwig VIII of Hesse-Darmstadt. Autograph score. Berlin, State Library.

1

3

60145-D.

GRADUS
AD
PARNASSUM,
Sive
MANUDUCTIO
AD
COMPOSITIONEM MUSICÆ
REGULAREM,
Methodo novâ, ac certâ, nondum antè
tam exacto ordine in lucem edita :

Elaborata à
JOANNE JOSEPHO FUX,
Sacræ Cæsareæ, ac Regiæ Ca-
tholicæ Majestatis CAROLI VI. Ro-
manorum Imperatoris
SUPREMO CHORI PRÆFECTO.

VIENNÆ AUSTRIÆ,
Typis Joannis Petri Van Ghelen , Sac. Cæs. Regiæque Catholicæ Majestatis Aulæ-Typographi , 1725.

2

Der
GENERAL-BASS
in der
COMPOSITION,
Oder:
Neue und gründliche
Anweisung,
Wie
Ein Music-Liebender mit besonderm Vortheil, durch
die Principia der Composition, nicht allein den General-Baß
im Kirchen-Cammer- und Theatralischen Stylo vollkommen, & in altiori
da erlernen; sondern auch zu gleicher Zeit in der Composition selbst, wichtige
Profectus machen könne.
Nebst einer Einleitung
Oder
Musicalischen Raisonnement
von der Music überhaupt, und vielen besondern
Materien der heutigen Praxeos.
Herausgegeben
von
Johann David Heinichen,
Königl. Pohln. und Churfl. Sächf. Capellmeister.
In Dreßten bey dem Autore zu finden 1728.

4

(1) and (2) Engraved frontispiece and title-page to the *Gradus ad Parnassum* by J. J. Fux, Vienna, 1725, the most widely-read theoretical work of the eighteenth century.   (3) Portrait of the author Johann Joseph Fux (1660–1741) (see fig. 1, p. 248), Hofkapellmeister and composer in Vienna.   Lithograph by H. E. Winther, 1821.   (4) Title-page to *Generalbass in der Composition* by Johann David Heinichen (1683–1729), Electoral Hofkapellmeister at Dresden.   Dresden, 1728 (first impression, 1711), a work reputed to be the best guide to a knowledge of thorough-bass.

1

Musicalisches
LEXICON
Oder
Musicalische Bibliothec,

Darinnen nicht allein
Die Musici, welche so wol in alten als
neuern Zeiten, ingleichen bey verschiedenen Natio-
nen, durch Theorie und Praxin sich hervor gethan, und was
von jedem bekannt worden, oder er in Schrifften hinter-
lassen, mit allem Fleisse und nach den vornehmsten
Umständen angeführet,
Sondern auch
Die in Griechischer, Lateinischer, Italiänischer und
Frantzösischer Sprache gebräuchliche Musicalische Kunst-
oder sonst dahin gehörige Wörter,
nach Alphabetischer Ordnung
vorgetragen und erkläret,
Und zugleich
die meisten vorkommende Signaturen
erläutert werden
von
Johann Gottfried Walthern,
Fürstl. Sächs. Hof-Musico und Organisten an der Haupt-Pfarr-Kirche
zu St. Petri und Pauli in Weimar.

Leipzig,
verlegts Wolffgang Deer, 1732.

2

3

4

(1) Johann Gottfried Walther (1684–1748), a friend of Sebastian Bach, organ composer, municipal and court organist at Weimar and writer on music. Oil painting in the Liceo Musicale di Bologna. (2) Title-page to Walther's fundamental *Musikalisches Lexikon*, Leipzig, 1732. (Mattheson's hand-written copy in the possession of the State Library, Berlin.) (3) Engraved frontispiece from Walther's *Lexicon*, showing a musical performance in a church. (4) Johann Kuhnau conducting a performance in the Thomaskirche at Leipzig (see p. 179). Engraved frontispiece to *Unfehlbare Engel-Freude oder Geistliches Gesang-Buch*, Leipzig, 1710.

I

2   3

(1) Birthplace of Johann Sebastian Bach (1685–1750) in the Frauenplan at Eisenach.   (2) Bach's father, Ambrosius Bach (1645–95), town musician of Eisenach. Oil painting of *c.* 1690 (from the effects of Carl Philipp Emanuel Bach), in the Music Department of the State Library, Berlin.   (3) Johann Sebastian Bach in early life. Unsigned oil painting in the Town Museum at Erfurt. Photograph by E. Bissinger.

I

2

3

(**1**) Johann Sebastian Bach, aged about thirty-five (1720). Oil painting by Johann Jacob Ihle in the Bach-House Museum at Eisenach. (**2**) Portrait of Bach in his old age (1746). Oil painting by Elias Gottlieb Haussmann (from the Thomas-schule) in the Stadtgeschichtliche Museum at Leipzig. (**3**) Chaconne (*Ciaconna*), variations on a ground bass, from the D minor Partita (No. 4) for violin alone. Autograph copy (*c.* 1730) by Bach's second wife Anna Magdalena, *née* Wülken, in the State Library, Berlin.

Johann Sebastian Bach: Prelude and Fugue in B minor for organ, Leipzig (c. 1740). First music page of the autograph manuscript, which is one of the most beautiful of all that have been preserved. Formerly in the Heyer Museum, Cologne.

1

2

Works of J. S. Bach in contemporary printed editions: (**1**) Canonic variations on the Christmas hymn: *Vom Himmel hoch da komm' ich her*, 'vor die Orgel mit 2 Clavieren und dem Pedal,' Nuremberg, 1746, Balthasar Schmid. (Composed by Bach for his admission to the Leipzig Musical Society.)   (**2**) *Musikalisches Opfer Sr. Kgl. Majestät in Preussen gewidmet* (fugues and canons on a theme of Frederick the Great), Leipzig, 1747.   Engraved by J. G. Schübler.

(**1**) Erdmann Neumeister (1671–1756), chief pastor of the Johanniskirche in Hamburg from 1715 and author of the texts for Bach's choral cantatas. Engraving by C. Fritzsch. (**2**) Interior of the Thomaskirche in Leipzig at the beginning of the eighteenth century. Engraved title-page to *Unfehlbare Engel-Freude oder Geistliches Gesang-Buch*, Leipzig, 1710. (See fig. 4, p. 255.) (**3**) Thomaskirche and Thomasschule, Leipzig. Engraving by Krügner (from the *Ratsordnung der Schule zu S. Thomae*, Leipzig, 1723). (**4**) Gottfried Reiche (1667–1734), council musician of Leipzig, with a 'Jäger trumpet' in the form of a posthorn, used for clarino parts. Engraving by C. F. Rosbach (1727), after the oil painting of E. G. Haussmann in the Stadtbibliothek, Leipzig.

(1) Wilhelm Friedemann Bach (1710–84), eldest son of Johann Sebastian Bach, known as the 'Halle Bach.'   Red chalk drawing by P. Gülle (1782) in the State Library, Berlin.   (2) Carl Philipp Emanuel Bach (1714–88), second surviving son of Bach, known as the 'Berlin' or 'Hamburg' Bach.   Unsigned engraving, after the pastel portrait by Gottlieb Friedrich Bach.   (3) Engraved title to the pianoforte sonatas, Op. 5, of Johann Christian Bach, London (c. 1770). Engraving by Bartolozzi, after G. B. Cipriani.   (4) Johann Christian Bach (1735–82), youngest son of J. S. Bach, known as the 'Milanese' or 'English' Bach.   Oil portrait by Thomas Gainsborough in the Liceo Musicale di Bologna.

(1) The supposed birthplace of Georg Friedrich Handel (1685–1759) at Halle-an-der-Saale (Großer Schlamm, No. 4).
(2) Handel seated at the harpsichord, composing. Oil portrait by Philipp Mercier in the possession of P. Clemen of
Bonn. (Another version of Lord Malmesbury's portrait at Heron Court.)   (3) Oil portrait by Thomas Hudson, London,
1749, which Handel took with him on his last visit to Germany to present to his relatives in Halle.   Hamburg, University
and State Library.   Photograph by Dr. P. Wolff, Frankfort.   (4) The Handel memorial erected in Westminster Abbey,
London, in 1762.   Standing figure in marble (with use of the death mask) by Louis François Roubiliac.

(1) The great firework display to celebrate the treaty of Aix-la-Chapelle in the Green Park, London, on 27th April 1749, for which occasion Handel wrote his *Fireworks Music* for wind-band. Contemporary English engraving. (2) Handel's *Salve regina* for soprano and string orchestra (*c.* 1710).   Autograph score in the State Library, Berlin.

I

2

3

4

(**1**) English chamber organ by Daniel Prior, 1786. London, Victoria and Albert Museum. (**2**) Handel among his players and singers at an oratorio performance. Contemporary drawing. London, British Museum. (**3**) The King's Theatre in the Haymarket, London's opera house in the time of Handel. Unsigned contemporary engraving. (**4**) Baroque church organ of the Handel period. Drawing by Adolf Menzel (woodcut from Franz Kugler's *Geschichte Friedrichs des Grossen*, Leipzig, 1840).

(1) From Handel's organ concerto in G minor (Op. 4, No. 3 of the edition published by J. Walsh, London, 1738). Autograph score in the British Museum, London. 2 to 4, Members of Handel's circle. (2) Thomas Morell (1703–84), librettist of Handel's oratorios *Judas Maccabaeus* and *Joshua*. Etching by James Basire, after Hogarth. (3) James Brydges, Earl of Carnarvon, Duke of Chandos (d. 1744), whose chapel-master Handel was from 1718 to 1721. Engraving by Reading, after Dahl. (4) Aaron Hill (1685–1750), poet and author, who, as director of the Haymarket Theatre, was the first to produce a Handel opera (*Rinaldo*) in London (1711). Engraving by H. Hulsbergh, 1709.

I

2

3

English caricatures from the time of Handel: (**1**) 'The Enraged Musician' (in the window, the conductor of the Italian opera in London, Gaetano Pugnani) (see fig. 1, p. 213). Engraving by Hogarth. (**2**) Caricature of Handel at the organ. Engraving after the caricature by Goupy. (**3**) Caricature of the chorus-singers at the performance of *Judith* (by William de Fesch, London, 1731). Etching by Hogarth.

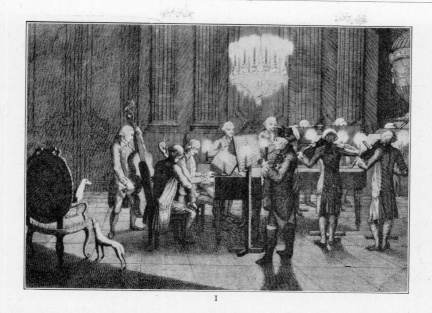

I

2

(**1**) Frederick the Great (1712–40–86) playing a flute concerto. Engraving by P. Haas. (**2**) The concert hall in the castle of Sans Souci at Potsdam. In the foreground: Hammerflügel (modern grand piano) by Gottfried Silbermann (see fig. 2, p. 235). Photograph by the Staatliche Bildstelle, Berlin.

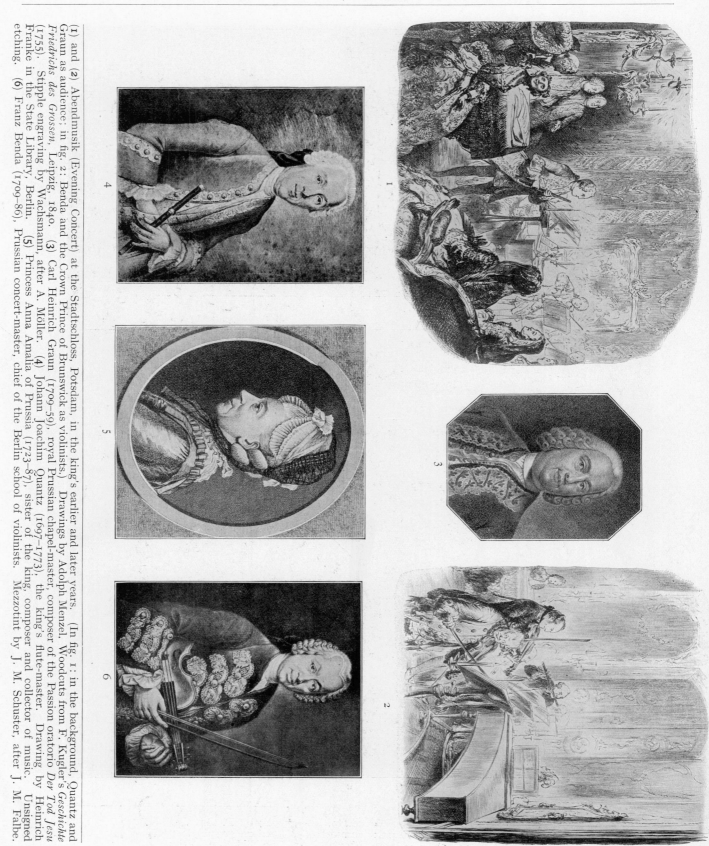

(1) and (2) Abendmusik (Evening Concert) at the Stadtschloss, Potsdam, in the king's earlier and later years. (In fig. 1: in the background, Quantz and Graun as audience; in fig. 2: Benda and the Crown Prince of Brunswick as violinists.) Drawings by Adolph Menzel. Woodcuts from F. Kugler's *Geschichte Friedrichs des Grossen*, Leipzig, 1840. (3) Carl Heinrich Graun (1709–59), royal Prussian chapel-master, composer of the Passion oratorio *Der Tod Jesu* (1755). Stipple engraving by Wachsmann, after A. Möller. (4) Johann Joachim Quantz (1697–1773), the king's flute-master. Drawing by Heinrich Franke in the State Library, Berlin. (5) Princess Anna Amalia of Prussia (1723–87), sister of the king, composer and collector of music. Unsigned etching. (6) Franz Benda (1709–86), Prussian concert-master, chief of the Berlin school of violinists. Mezzotint by J. M. Schuster, after J. M. Falbe.

1

2

3

(1) The dancer Barberina (Barbara Campanini), by marriage Gräfin Cocceji (1721–99). Pastel portrait by Rosalba Carriera in the Dresden Gallery. Museum photograph. (2) The opera-singer Gertrud Elisabeth Mara, *née* Schmeling (1749–1833), attached to the Berlin Opera House from 1771. Stipple engraving by Rauch. (3) Aria from the opera *Cleofide* by J. A. Hasse (Dresden, 1731), with coloratura passages for the singer Porporino (Anton Huber, *Ital.* Antonio Uberti), in Frederick the Great's own hand. Berlin, State Library.

(1) Bust of Christoph Willibald von Gluck (1714–87) by Jean Antoine Houdon, Paris, 1775.   Painted plaster cast in the Kaiser Friedrich Museum, Berlin.   (Sent to the court of Berlin by the artist.   The marble bust, executed in 1777, was destroyed in the fire at the Paris Opera in 1873.)   (2) Gluck, oil portrait by Jean Baptiste Greuze in the Musée du Louvre, Paris.   (Bequeathed by E. A. Montmartel, d. 1907.)   Photograph by Les archives photographiques.   (3) Gluck with his wife Marianne, née Pergin.   Unsigned oil portrait (c. 1772), in the possession of the Gluck family, now in the Vienna Historical Museum.   Photograph by Dr. P. Wolff, Frankfort.

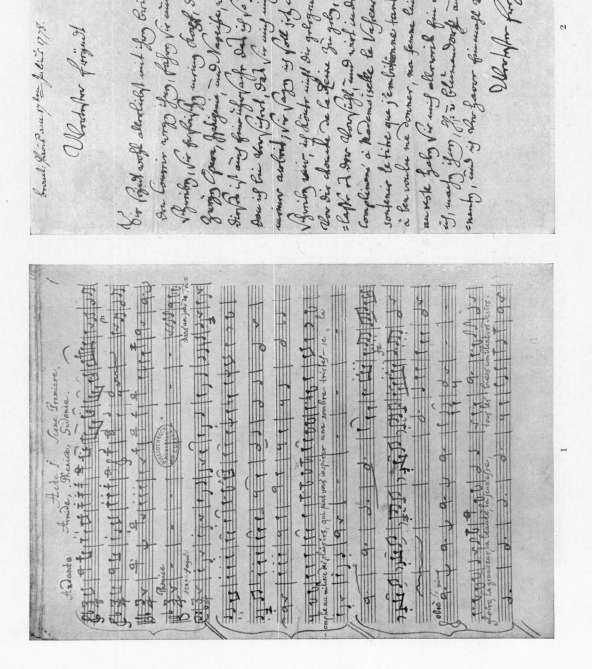

Gluck: (1) Opening of the first act of the opera *Armide* (Paris, 1777, text by Philippe Quinault). Page 1 from the fragment (Act i, scs. 1–4) that has been preserved of the autograph score. Paris, Bibliothèque de l'Opéra. (2) Autograph letter to the secretary of embassy in Paris, Franz Kruthoffer, Vienna, 28th June 1778. Formerly in the Heyer Museum, Cologne.

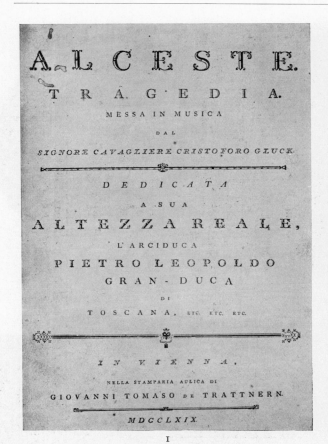

1

2

3

(1) Gluck: Title-page to the printed score of the opera *Alceste* (Vienna, 1767, text by Raniero di Calsabigi), with the dedicatory epistle setting forth the composer's attempts at reform. Published in Vienna, 1769, by J. T. von Trattnern. (2) Georg Matthias Monn (1717–50), a predecessor of Haydn as an instrumental composer. Minuet from the autograph score of the D major symphony, 1740. Vienna, Nationalbibliothek. (3) Gottlieb Muffat (1690–1770), organist to the imperial court and pianoforte composer. Engraved title to the *Componimenti Musicali per il Cembalo*, Augsburg, 1739, containing six suites and a *Ciacona con 38 variazioni*. Engraving by J. A. Fridrich.

(1) Birthplace of Joseph Haydn (1737–1809), at Rohrau-an-der-Leitha, in Lower Austria. Water-colour by Mayenberg (c. 1825). Vienna, Museum der Gesellschaft der Musikfreunde. 2 to 4, Portraits of Haydn: (2) Engraving by J. E. Mansfeld, Vienna, 1781. (3) Stipple engraving by Scheffner, 1805, reversed copy of C. Pfeiffer's engraving, after V. G. Kininger's drawing of 1799. (4) Stipple engraving by Thomas Hardy, London, 1792. (5) Prince Nicolaus Joseph Esterhazy (1714–90), Haydn's patron and employer. Engraving by Georg Friedrich Schmidt (Petersburg, 1759), after J. L. Tocqué (1758).

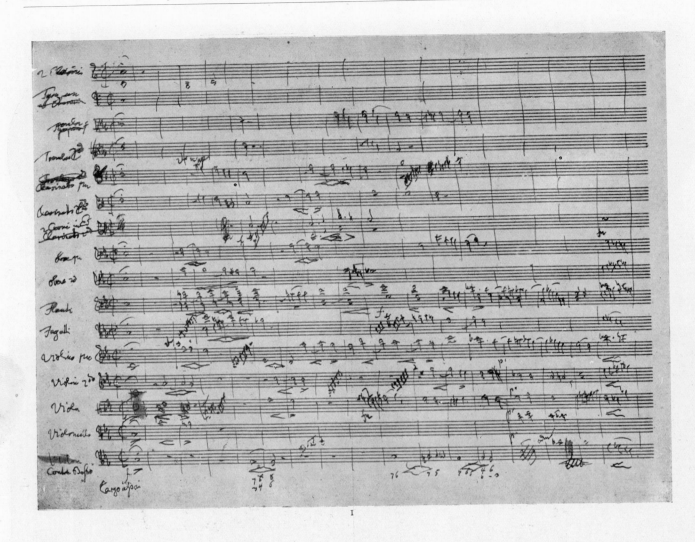

1

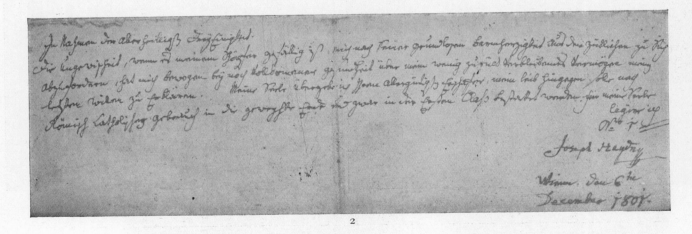

2

Haydn: (1) Autograph score (sketch) for the introduction (Representation of Chaos) to the oratorio *The Creation*, 1797. Vienna, National Library. (2) Closing paragraph (codicil) to the will that had been drawn up on 5th May 1801. Vienna, 6th December 1801. Vienna, National Library.

(1) Announcement of the first public performance (following the original one on 29th–30th April 1798, at the Schwarzenberg Palace) of Haydn's oratorio *The Creation* at the Burgtheater, Vienna, on 19th March 1799. (2) Johann Michael Haydn (1737–1806), Joseph's younger brother, director of the archbishop's orchestra and organist to the cathedral at Salzburg. Stipple engraving by J. F. Schröter. (3) Gottfried Baron van Swieten (1734–1803), director of the Imperial Hofbibliothek, Vienna; a friend of Haydn, Mozart, and young Beethoven, and editor of the texts of Haydn's *Creation* and *The Seasons*. Engraving by J. E. Mansfeld, after J. C. von Lakner. (4) Johann Georg Albrechtsberger (1736–1809), organist to the imperial court and chapel-master of the Stephanskirche, Vienna. Composer and theorist. Stipple engraving by J. Neidl, after Stainhauser von Treuberg. (5) Johann Peter Salomon (1745–1815), violinist and concert impresario, who persuaded Haydn to undertake the two visits to England (1790–2 and 1794–5). Stipple engraving by G. S. Facius (London, 1807), after William Owen. (6) Abt Maximilian Stadler (1748–1833), church composer; a friend of Haydn and of Mozart. Engraving by J. B. Pfitzer, 1817.

1   2

3

(**1**) Carl Ditters von Dittersdorf (1739–99), after Haydn and Mozart the most important Austrian instrumental composer of his time. Engraving by C. T. Riedel. (**2**) Engraved title to Haydn's three symphonies, Op. 38, dedicated to Prince Nicolaus Esterhazy, Vienna, 1787, Artaria & Co. (**3**) Opening page of the autograph score of Dittersdorf's piano concerto in A, 1779. Berlin, State Library.

(1) and (3) Two medallion impressions of Joseph Haydn by N. Gatteaux (1 commemorating the first performance of *The Creation* in Paris, 1800) and of Carl Leberecht (commissioned by the Philharmonic Society of St. Petersburg in 1802). Vienna, Gesellschaft der Musikfreunde. (2) Joseph Bonno (1710–88), composer and chapel-master to the imperial court. Unsigned engraving. (4) Florian Leopold Gassmann (1729–74), imperial chapel-master and founder of the 'Tonkünstlersozietät.' Engraving by J. Balzer, after Anton Hickel. (5) Emanuel Aloys Förster (1748–1823), instrumental composer. Lithograph by Josef Teltscher. (6) Joseph Starzer (1726–87), composer of ballet. Stipple engraving by Putz. (7) Anton Eberl (1766–1807), instrumental composer, a friend of Mozart. Etching by Rahl, after F. Jagemann. (8) Franz Asplmayer (1721–86?), composer of ballet and chamber-music. Unsigned pencil drawing. Berlin, State Library. (9) Abt Joseph Gelinek (1758–1825), fashionable composer of piano music. Engraving by F. John, after L. Letronne.

1   2   3

4   5

(**1**) Leopold Mozart (1719–87), Hofkompositeur and vice-chapelmaster to the archbishops of Salzburg, father of Wolfgang. Unsigned oil portrait (*c.* 1760). Salzburg, Mozart Museum. (**2**) Maria Anna Mozart, *née* Pertlin (1720–78), Wolfgang's mother. Unsigned oil portrait of *c.* 1770. Salzburg, Mozart Museum. (**3**) Wolfgang Amadeus Mozart (1756–91) as à youth, at the harpsichord. Oil painting by the Swiss painter Thadäus Helbling (Rome, 1770?), loan presentation to the Mozart Museum, Salzburg. (**4**) Wolfgang's birthplace at Salzburg, Getreidegasse 9. (**5**) Papa Mozart with his children Wolfgang and Marianne in Paris. Engraving by J. B. Delafosse, 1764, after the water-colour by L. C. de Carmontelle painted in November 1763 (in the Musée de Chantilly).

I

2

3

4   5

(**1**) Tea-party at Prince Conti's in the Temple, Paris (with the eleven-year-old Mozart at the harpsichord).   Part of the oil painting by M. Barth. Ollivier (Paris, 1766) in the Musée du Louvre.   Photograph by Les Archives Photographiques. (**2**) Wolfgang's note added to his father's letter of congratulations to his friend and landlord Lorenz Hagenauer at Salzburg.   Bologna, 28th July 1770.   Berlin, State Library.   3 to 5, Portraits of Wolfgang: (**3**) Stipple engraving by J. Neidl after the bronze medallion struck by Leonard Posch in 1788–9.   (**4**) Young Mozart at the harpsichord.   Oil portrait by Cignaroli, painted in January 1770 at Verona.   In the possession of Dr. Karl Kupelwieser (formerly owned by Frau Therese Kammerlacher, *née* von Sonnleithner), in Vienna.   (**5**) Head taken from the unfinished oil painting by Mozart's brother-in-law, Joseph Lange (1782–3).   Salzburg, Mozart Museum.

I

2

Autograph music by W. A. Mozart: (1) Beginning of the piano rondo in D major (Köchel-Verzeichnis No. 485), composed on 10th January 1786. Formerly in the Heyer Museum, Cologne. (2) Aria of Sarastro *In diesen heil'gen Hallen*, from the second act of the opera *The Magic Flute*, 1791. Autograph score in the State Library, Berlin.

1

2

3

(**1**) Engraved title of Mozart's Six String Quartets, Op. 10 (Köchel-Verzeichnis, Nos. 387, 421, 428, 458, 464, 465), Vienna 1785, Artaria & Co.   (**2**) Theatre programme of the original performance of *The Magic Flute* on 30th September 1791, in the Imperial Theater auf der Wieden, Vienna.   (**3**) The two last pages from Mozart's autograph catalogue of his works, with entries from July to 15th November 1791 (Köchel-Verzeichnis, Nos. 620–623).

1

2

3

4

(1) Mozart's sons: Wolfgang Xaver (Amadeus) (1791–1844) and Carl (1784–1858). Oil painting by a Viennese artist, 1798. Salzburg, Mozart Museum. (2) Mozart's wife, Constanze, *née* Weber (1763–1842), wife of G. N. von Nissen by her second marriage (1809–26). Oil painting by Hans Hansen, Vienna, 1802. Salzburg, Mozart Museum. (3) Georg Nicolas von Nissen (1761–1826), Danish counsellor of state, second husband of Constanze Mozart. Lithograph from Nissen's biography of Mozart, 1828. (4) Scene (Temple of Wisdom) for Mozart's *Magic Flute* at the Kärntnertor Theatre, Vienna. Etching by N. Bittner, 1818, after Anton de Pian.

1

2

3

4

5

6

Members of Mozart's circle: (1) Anton Raaff (1714–97), opera-singer, for whom Mozart wrote the part of Idomeneo. Unsigned oil portrait. Bonn, Lese- und Erholungsgesellschaft. (2) Joseph Lange (1751–1831), imperial court actor, brother-in-law of Mozart through his marriage to Aloysia Weber. Stipple engraving by C. Pfeiffer (1795), after Lange's self-portrait. (3) Lorenzo da Ponte (Emanuele Conegliano, 1749–1838), librettist of Mozart's *Figaro*, *Don Giovanni*, and *Cosi fan tutte*. Stipple engraving after N. Rogers. (4) Emanuel Schikaneder (1751–1812), librettist of *The Magic Flute*. Etching by J. Löschenkohl. (5) Anna Storace (1766–1817), opera-singer, the first Susanna in Mozart's *Figaro*, 1786. Engraved silhouette by J. Löschenkohl. (6) C. Gottlieb Stephanie the Younger (1741–1800), librettist of Mozart's *Entführung* (*Seraglio*). Engraving by J. E. Mansfeld, after Joseph Lange.

South German composers: (1) Franz Xaver Richter (1709–89), member (chamber-composer) of the Mannheim court orchestra and from 1769 chapel-master of Strasburg Cathedral. Engraving by C. Guérin, 1785. (2) Johann Stamitz (1717–57), concert-master and chamber director to the elector of Mannheim, one of the founders of the modern style of instrumental music. Medallion portrait from the engraved title to the collection ' L'art du violon,' by J. B. Cartier, Paris, 1798. (3) Christian Cannabich (1731–98), Stamitz's successor as chamber director at Mannheim and Munich. Engraving by E. Verhelst, 1779. (4) Abt Georg Joseph Vogler (1749–1814), master of Carl Maria von Weber and Meyerbeer, finally chapel-master at Darmstadt. Stipple engraving by F. Dürmer, 1795. (5) Franz Xaver Sterkel (1750–1817), electoral music - director at Aschaffenburg. Stipple engraving, 1411. (6) Justin Heinrich Knecht (1752–1817), organist at Biberach, composer and theorist. Engraving by Schramm, Munich, 1803. (7) Peter von Winter (1754–1825), chapel-master at Munich, composer of the opera *Das unterbrochene Opferfest*, 1796. Unsigned engraving. (8) Johann Rudolpf Zumsteeg (1760–1802), chapel-master at Stuttgart, a forerunner of Schubert and Loewe as a song and ballad composer. Stipple engraving by C. F. Stoelzel (1799), after Hiemer.

Saxon–Thuringian composers: (1) Johann Heinrich Rolle (1718–85), municipal director of music at Magdeburg, church composer. Engraving by C. G. Geyser, after Fischer. (2) Maria Antonis Walpurgis, electoress of Saxony (1724–80), opera composer and author of cantata texts. Engraving by Giuseppe Canale, Dresden, 1764. (3) Georg Benda (1722–95), chapel-master at Gotha, composer of the melodrama *Ariadne auf Naxos*. Engraving by C. G. Geyser, after J. F. Mechau. (4) Ernst Wilhelm Wolf (1735–92), chapel-master at Weimar. Engraving by Liebe, after Heinsius. (5) Johann Adam Hiller (1728–1804), from 1789 cantor at the Thomaskirche, Leipzig, creator of the German Singspiel. Etching by C. G. Geyser (1770), after Füger. (6) Anton Schweitzer (1735–87), successor to Benda at Gotha, composer of the opera *Alceste* (text by Wieland). Engraving by Liebe, after Heinsius. (7) Johann Gottlieb Naumann (1741–1801), principal chapel-master to the elector at Dresden, reputable opera and church composer. Stipple engraving by Hüllmann, after Seydelmann. (8) Joseph Schuster (1748–1812), chapel-master at Dresden. Engraving by J. C. B. Gottschick (1811), after von Vieth (1796). (9) Franz Seydelmann (1748–1806), chapel-master at Dresden together with Schuster. Engraving by M. Thoenert (1782), after J. C. Berkeekamp.

(1) Christian Gottlob Neefe (1748–98), music director to the elector at Bonn, master of Beethoven. Engraving by Liebe, after Rosenberg. (2) Johann Wilhelm Hässler (1747–1822), piano composer at Erfurt and Moscow (see fig. 3, p. 247). Stipple engraving by Zetter, after J. F. Wagner. (3) Johann Abraham Peter Schulz (1747–1800), chapel-master at Copenhagen, opera and song composer. Stipple engraving by F. Jügel, 1794. (4) Johann Ladislaus Dussek (1760–1812), Bohemian piano virtuoso and composer. Crayon engraving by Jean Godefroy. (5) Johann Friedrich Reichardt (1752–1814), Prussian Hofkapellmeister, the most eminent song composer and writer on music of the eighteenth century. Engraving by B. H. Bendix (1796), after S. Henry (1791). (6) Prince Louis Ferdinand of Prussia (1722–1806), nephew of Frederick the Great, esteemed by Beethoven as pianist and chamber composer. Mezzotint by A. Geiger, after the oil portrait by Joseph Grassi, Dresden, 1806. (7) August Eberhard Müller (1767–1817), cantor at the Thomaskirche, Leipzig, later chapel-master at Weimar. Stipple engraving by F. A. Brückner. (8) Friedrich Heinrich Himmel (1765–1814), Reichardt's successor as Hofkapellmeister in Berlin, composer of the Liederspiel *Fanchon, das Leiermädchen*, Berlin, 1804. Stipple engraving by F. Bolt (1803), after Lauer.

(**1**) Christoph Gottlob Schröder (1699–1782).   Engraving by J. C. Sysang.   (**2**) Friedrich Wilhelm Marpurg (1718–95). Stipple engraving by F. W. Bollinger.   (**3**) Christian Friedrich Daniel Schubart (1739–61).   Engraving by E. Morace, after A. F. Oehlenhainz, 1789 (oil portrait in the Gemäldegalerie, Stuttgart).   (**4**) Martin Gerbert (1720–93), Prince Abbot of the Benedictine monastery of St. Blasien im Schwarzwald.   Engraving by C. W. Bock, 1786.   (**5**) Johann Philipp Kirnberger (1721–83).   Stipple engraving by F. W. Bollinger.   (**6**) Johann Georg Sulzer (1720–79).   Engraving by J. F. Bause, after Anton Graff.   (**7**) Ernst Ludwig Gerber (1746–1819).   Engraving by A. Brückner, after F. W. Bollinger, 1797.   (**8**) Johann Nicolaus Forkel (1749–1818).   Engraving by C. T. Riedel, 1813, after Bornemann, 1786.   (**9**) Ernst Floris Friedrich Chladni (1756–1827).   Stipple engraving by F. W. Bollinger.

(1) Johann Ulrich Haffner (d. 1767), lutanist and music publisher at Nuremberg. Engraving by J. W. Störr, 1730. (2) Johann André (1741–99), 'Singspiel' and song composer, founder of the publishing firm at Offenbach-am-Main (1784). Engraving by D. Berger (1780), after J. C. Frisch. (3) Anton André (1775–1842), son and successor of the above, the acquirer of the Mozart manuscripts. Unsigned lithograph. (4) Bernard Christoph Breitkopf (1695–1777), founder of the book printing and publishing firm of Breitkopf & Härtel in Leipzig (1719). Engraving by G. G. Endner, after E. Gottlob. (5) Johann Gottlieb Immanuel Breitkopf (1719–94), son of the above, who inherited the business and improved music-printing types. Engraving by S. Halle, 1793. (6) Gottfried Christopf Härtel (1763–1827). Entered the Breitkopf firm in 1795; a modern music publisher in the grand style. After an oil painting by F. G. Waldmüller (in the possession of Breitkopf & Härtel). (7) Franz Anton Hoffmeister (1754–1812), composer and music publisher, who, together with Ambrosius Kühnel, founded the 'Bureau de musique' at Leipzig in 1800, which eventually developed into the firm of C. F. Peters. Stipple engraving by F. W. Nettling, after Lauer. (8) Anton Diabelli (1781–1858), composer and Viennese music publisher, principal publisher of Schubert's works. Lithograph by J. Kriehuber, Vienna, 1841. (9) Hans Georg Nägeli (1773–1836), composer and music publisher at Zurich. Lithograph by J. Billeter, 1829.

1

2

3

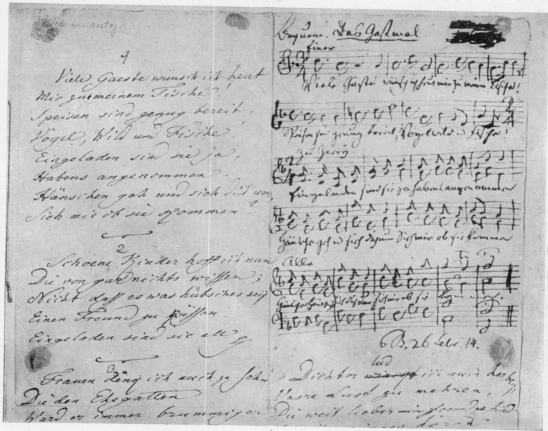

4

(**1**) Carl Fasch (1736–1800), founder of the Berliner Singakademie, 1792, who thus prepared the way for a great new era in the study of choral music in Germany.   Engraving by C. T. Riedel, after W. von Schadow.   (**2**) Carl Friedrich Zelter (1758–1832), song composer, succeeded his master Fasch as director of the Singakademie and founded the first 'liedertafel,' 1809.   Lithograph by L. Heine, after the oil painting by Carl Begas, 1827 (in the Goethe National Museum at Weimar).   (**3**) Carl Friedrich Rungenhagen (1778–1851), Zelter's successor as director of the Singakademie.   Lithograph by François Legrand after Henning.   (**4**) *Das Gastmahl*.   Song by Goethe (*Offne Tafel*; Weimar, 12th October 1813), set to music by his friend Zelter (Berlin, 26th February 1814).   Autograph copy by both authors.   (After the copy published in Berlin in May 1832.)

(1) Birthplace of Ludwig van Beethoven (1770–1827), at Bonn, Bonngasse No. 515 (now No. 20).   Seen from the garden side.   Modern etching.   (2) The sixteen-year-old Beethoven as Kammermusikus to the elector of Cologne, after the lost silhouette by Neesen.   Reproduction in the biographical notes on Beethoven by F. G. Wegeler and Ferdinand Ries, Coblenz, 1838.   (3) Engraved title of Beethoven's first printed work, the three pianoforte sonatas dedicated to the elector Maximilian Friedrich, Speyer, 1783, Rat Bossler's publishing firm.   (4) Beethoven bust (with use of the face mask) by Franz Klein, Vienna 1812, in the possession of the Streicher family, Vienna.   Cast in the Beethoven House at Bonn.   (5) Oil portrait by Ferdinand Schimon, Vienna, 1818–19.   Bonn, Beethoven House.

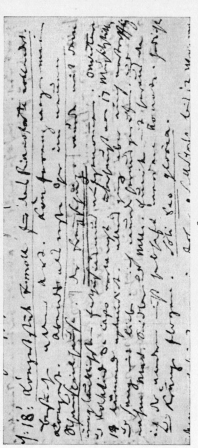

(1) Carl Maria von Weber's home at Klein-Hosterwitz, near Dresden; the 'summer nest' in Felsner the vine-dresser's house where the composer spent his summers from 1818 onward. Lithograph from a drawing by F. T. Brauer. (2) Entry describing the great success of the first performance of *Der Freischütz* (Berlin, 18th June 1821) in Weber's own diary, now in the possession of the von Weber family in Dresden. (3) The opera-singer Henriette Sontag (by marriage Countess Rossi, 1806–54) as Agatha in Weber's *Freischütz*. Mezzotint by Reynolds (London, 1829), after N. L. F. Gosse.

1

3

4

2

5

6

(1) Carl Maria von Weber as conductor. Lithograph by J. Hayter, London, 1826. (2) The old Hoftheater in Dresden, where Weber was director of the newly-organized German opera. Water-colour in the City Museum, Dresden. (3) Ernst Theodor Amadeus (Wilhelm) Hoffmann (1776–1822), composer of the opera *Undine* (Berlin, 1816), and a witty writer on music. Unsigned lithograph. (4) Heinrich Marschner (1795–1861), composer of the opera *Hans Heiling* (Berlin, 1833). Lithograph by M. Gauci after F. A. Jung. (5) Conradin Kreutzer (1780–1849), composer of the opera *Das Nachtlager von Granada* (Vienna, 1834). Lithograph by Joseph Kriehuber (Vienna, 1837). (6) Albert Lortzing (1801–51), composer of the opera *Der Wildschütz* (Leipzig, 1842). Lithograph by G. Schlick, 1845.

Pianoforte virtuosos and composers: (1) Johann Nepomuk Hummel (1778–1837). Lithograph by Vigneron. (2) Carl Czerny (1791–1857). Lithograph by Joseph Kriehuber, Vienna, 1833. (3) John Field (1782–1837). Unsigned lithograph. (4) Sigismund Thalberg (1812–71). Unsigned engraving. (5) Stephen Heller (1814–88). Oil portrait by Louis Gustave Ricard. Paris, Musée du Louvre. Photograph by Les Archives photographiques. (6) Henri Litolff (1818–91). Lithograph by Joseph Kriehuber, Vienna, 1848. (7) Henri Herz (1803–88). Lithograph by P. L. H. Grévedon, Paris, 1837. (8) Ignaz Moscheles (1794–1870). Lithograph by A. Brandt, 1849. (9) Adolf Henselt (1814–89). Lithograph by A. Grahl.

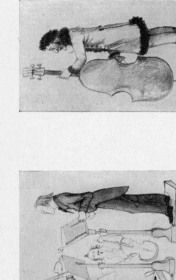

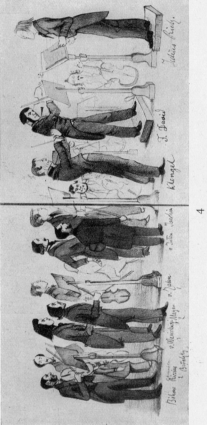

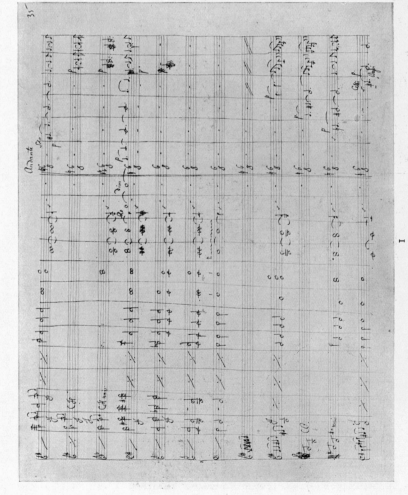

(1) End of the first movement and bridge passage leading into the second, from the violin concerto (E minor, Op. 64, written 1844) by Felix Mendelssohn-Bartholdy (1809–47). Page 35 of the autograph score in the State Library, Berlin. (2) Felix Mendelssohn. Engraving by J. Caspar, after the oil painting by Mendelssohn's brother-in-law, Wilhelm Hensel. (3) to (5) Members of the Gewandhaus orchestra, Leipzig, under Julius Rietz (1812–77), who succeeded Mendelssohn and Gade as conductor. (3) The bassoonist Carl Wilhelm von Inten (1799–1877). (4) First violins (David, Klengel, Joachim, etc.), rehearsing the *presto* passage in Beethoven's *Leonora Overture No. 3*. (5) The double-bass player Johann Friedrich Peglow (1790–1868). Lithographs after the humorous sketches by the violoncellist Christian Riemers (Leipzig, c. 1850).

1

2

3

4

Lithograph title-pages to music printed in the middle of the nineteenth century.   (1) Music to Sophocles' *Antigone* by Felix Mendelssohn-Bartholdy, Op. 55.   Leipzig, F. Kistner.   Drawing by Julius Hübner, 1842.   (2) Piano score of the oratorio *Elias* by Mendelssohn, Op. 70.   Bonn, N. Simrock.   Drawing by Julius Hübner, 1847, lithograph print by C. Hahn.   (3) *Hausmusik* (fifty songs by German poets) by Wilhelm Heinrich Riehl, Stuttgart, 1855.   J. G. Cotta. Cover design by Ludwig Richter.   (4) *Spanische Lieder* by Hermann Krigar (Menzel's brother-in-law), dedicated to Mme Pauline Viardot-Garcia.   Leipzig, 1866, G. Heinze.   Pen drawing by Adolph Menzel.

(**1**) Birthplace of Robert Schumann (1810–56), at Zwickau in Saxony. Steel engraving by A. Krausse. (**2**) to (**5**) Portraits of Schumann: (**2**) Youthful portrait of *c.* 1834. Painting over a pastel. Zwickau, Schumann Museum (in the König Albert Museum). (**3**) Lithograph of Joseph Kriehuber, Vienna, 1839. (**4**) Robert and Clara Schumann. Double relief by Ernst Rietschel, Dresden, 1848. (**5**) Hamburg daguerreotype on 20th March 1850. (**6**) Song, *Du bist wie eine Blume* (by Heine, No. 24, from the song-cycle *Myrthen*, Op. 25, written in 1840). Autograph copy with the dedication 'Meiner Clara' ('To my Clara'). Zwickau, Schumann Museum.

(1) Schumann's father-in-law, the piano teacher Friedrich Wieck (1785–1873). Photograph, 1869. (2) The composer Ludwig Schunke, a friend of Schumann's youth (1810–34), on his deathbed. After a drawing by Emil Kirchner. (3) Schumann's wife, Clara Wieck, the famous pianist (1819–96) as fiancée. Drawing by Elvire Leyser, *née* Härtel, Maxen, near Dresden, 1836 (see also fig. 1, p. 344). Zwickau, Schumann Museum. (4) View of the Robert Schumann room in the Schumann Museum, Zwickau. In the foreground the Hammerflügel (grand piano) by Andreas Stein, Vienna, 1827, the instrument used by Clara Wieck at her first appearance in the Leipzig Gewandhaus on 20th October 1828. Photograph by Dr. P. Wolff, Frankfort (from the 'Musik im Leben der Völker' Exhibition, Frankfort, 1927).

(**1**) Andreas Romberg (1761–1821), composer of Schiller's *Lied von der Glocke*.   Engraving, 1810.   (**2**) Friedrich Schneider, composer of the oratorio *Das Weltgericht*.   Unsigned lithograph.   (**3**) Franz Lachner (1803–90), composer of the eight orchestral suites.   Steel engraving by Christian Riedt.   Masters of song-writing: (**4**) Friedrich Silcher (1789–1860). Unsigned lithograph.   (**5**) Carl Loewe (1796–1869), master of the ballad.   Lithograph, after the oil portrait by Most.   (**6**) Robert Franz (1815–92).   Unsigned etching.   (**7**) Ferdinand Hiller (1811–85).   Lithograph by E. Kühnel. (**8**) Robert Volkmann (1815–83).   Tinted photograph (so-called salifiable base) from *c*. 1855.   (**9**) Max Bruch (1838–1920). Photograph by Reichard and Lindner, Berlin.

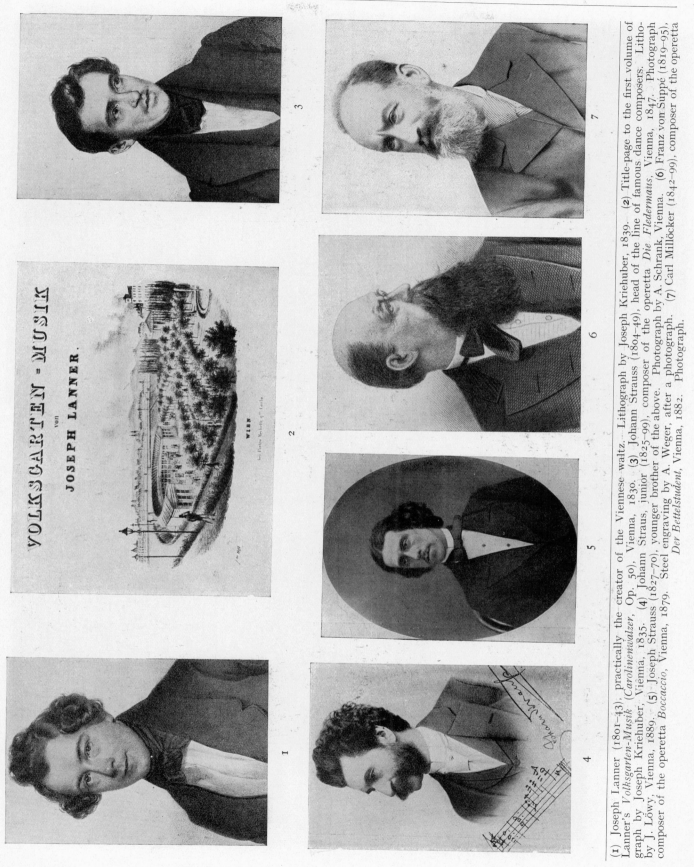

(1) Joseph Lanner (1801–43), practically the creator of the Viennese waltz.—Lithograph by Joseph Kriehuber, 1839.— (2) Title-page to the first volume of Lanner's *Volksgarten-Musik* (*Carolinenwalzer*, Op. 50), Vienna, 1830. (3) Johann Strauss (1804–49), head of the line of famous dance composers. Lithograph by Joseph Kriehuber, Vienna, 1835. (4) Johann Strauss, junior (1825–99), composer of the operetta *Die Fledermaus*, Vienna, 1847. Photograph by J. Löwy, Vienna, 1889. (5) Joseph Strauss (1827–70), younger brother of the above. Photograph by A. Schrank, Vienna.   (6) Franz von Suppé (1819–95), composer of the operetta *Boccaccio*, Vienna, 1879.   Steel engraving by A. Weger, after a photograph.   (7) Carl Millöcker (1842–99), composer of the operetta *Der Bettelstudent*, Vienna, 1882.   Photograph.

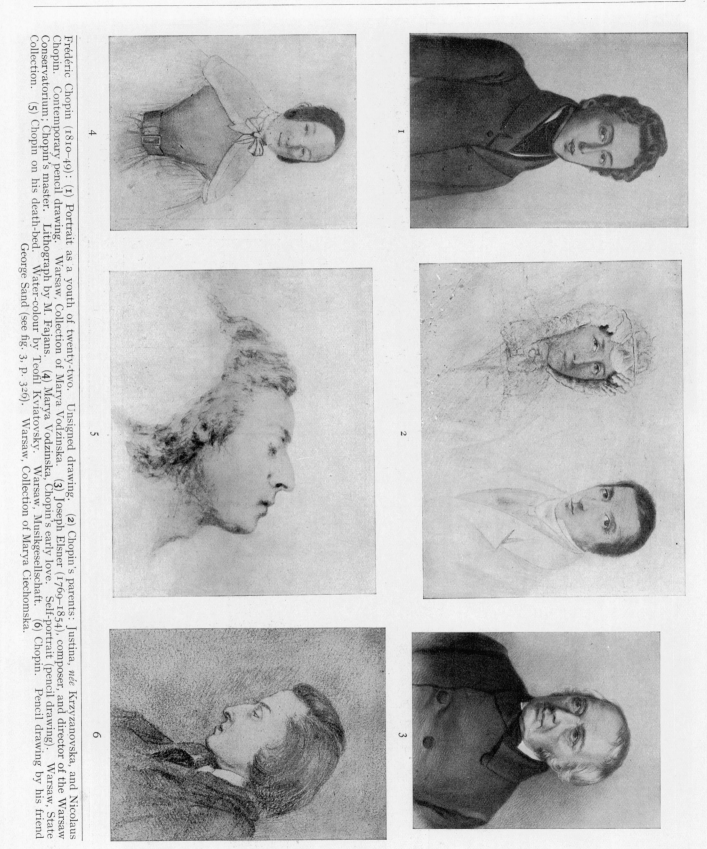

Frédéric Chopin (1810–49): (1) Portrait as a youth of twenty-two. Unsigned drawing. (2) Chopin's parents: Justina, née Krzyzanovska, and Nicolaus Chopin. Contemporary pencil drawing. Warsaw, Collection of Marya Vodzinska. (3) Joseph Elsner (1769–1854), composer, and director of the Warsaw Conservatorium; Chopin's master. Lithograph by M. Fajans. (4) Marya Vodzinska, Chopin's early love. Self-portrait (pencil drawing). Warsaw State Conservatorium; Chopin's master. Water-colour by Teofil Kviatovsky. Warsaw, Musikgesellschaft. (6) Chopin. Pencil drawing by his friend Collection. (5) Chopin on his death-bed. George Sand (see fig. 3, p. 326). Warsaw, Collection of Marya Ciechomska.

1

2

3

Frédéric Chopin (1810–49): (1) Oil portrait by Eugène Delacroix. Paris, Musée du Louvre. From the Marmontel Bequest. Photograph by Les Archives photographiques. (2) Oil painting by Antoni Kolberg, 1848. Warsaw, Musikgesellschaft. (3) Beginning of the Scherzo from the B flat minor piano sonata, Op. 35 (with the Funeral March); autograph copy of 1839. Leipzig, Breitkopf & Härtel.

Hector Berlioz (1803–69): (**1**) Oil portrait by Gustave Courbet (1850) in the Musée du Louvre, Paris. Photograph by Les Archives photographiques. (**2**) Oil portrait by Honoré Daumier (*c*. 1860) in the Musée de Versailles. Photograph by J. E. Bulloz, Paris. (**3**) 'Un Bal. Valse,' the second movement of the *Symphonie fantastique* (*Episode de la vie d'un artiste*, Op. 14). From the autograph score in the Bibliothèque du Conservatoire, Paris. (**4**) Félicien David (1810–76), composer of the symphonic ode *Le Désert*, Paris, 1844. Engraving by Metzmacher, 1858. (**5**) Ernest Reyer (1823–1909), composer of the opera *Sigurd*, Brussels, 1884. Engraving by P. Cathelain.

(**1**) François Antoine Habeneck (1781–1849), conductor of the Paris Conservatoire concerts.   Etching by A. Masson.
(**2**) 'Un concours du Conservatoire' (c. 1875).   Engraving after D. Lancelot.   (**3**) Ambroise Thomas (1811–96), composer of the opera *Mignon*, Paris, 1866.   Crayon engraving by A. Nargeot, after Hippolyte Flandrin, 1852.   Charles
Gounod (1818–93), composer of the opera *Faust*, Paris, 1859.   (**4**) Gounod as a young man at the piano.   Pencil drawing
by Jean Ingres, Rome 1840, in the possession of Mme de Lassus, Paris.   (**5**) Oil portrait by Aug. Scheffer in the
Musée de Versailles.   Photograph by J. E. Bulloz, Paris.

1

2

3

4

5

Georges Bizet (1838–75), composer of the opera *Carmen*, Paris, 1875: (**1**) Oil portrait by F. H. Giacomotti (Rome, before 1860). (**2**) Opening page of the autograph score of *Carmen*. Paris, Collection of M. Strauss. (**3**) Edouard Lalo (1823–92), composer of the opera *Le roi d'Ys*, Paris, 1888. Etching after a photograph by Lejeune. (**4**) Léo Delibes (1836–91), composer of opera and ballet, *Coppélia*, Paris, 1870. Etching by Louise Abbema. (**5**) Jules Massenet (1842–1912), composer of the opera *Manon*, Paris, 1884. Lithograph by P. Maurou, after a photograph.

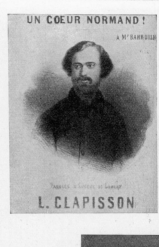

(1) Louis Clapisson (1806–66), composer of the operetta *La Fanchonette*, Paris, 1856. Lithograph. Title-page by Mouilleron, after Mlle E. Lothon. (2) Jacques Offenbach (1819–80), greatest of the French operetta writers, and composer of the comic opera *Les contes d'Hoffmann*, Paris, 1881. From a Paris photograph. (3) Louis Aimé Maillart (1817–71), composer of the comic opera *Les dragons de Villars*, Paris, 1856. Photograph by Pierre Petit. (4) Victor Massé (1822–84), composer of the comic opera *La reine Topaze*, Paris, 1856. Photograph by Pierre Petit. (5) Charles Lecoq (1832–1918), composer of the operetta *La fille de Madame Angot*, Paris, 1872. Photograph by Goupil & Cie. (6) Types in a theatre audience. Water-colour by Honoré Daumier.

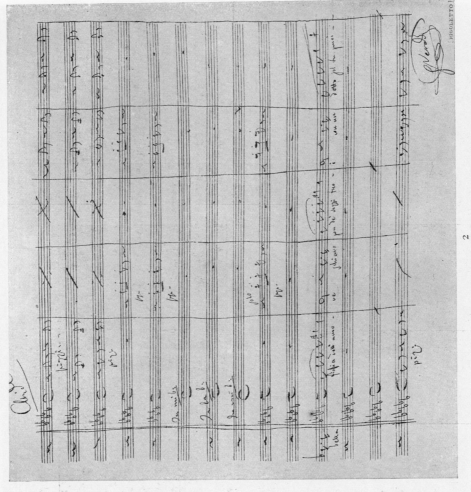

Giuseppe Verdi (1813–1901).   (1) Etching by C. Geoffroy, 1886.   (2) Extract (Duke: *Bella figlia dell' amore*) from the quartet in the third act (No. 16) of the opera *Rigoletto*, composed in 1850 (first performance, Venice, 1851). Autograph score in the archives of G. Ricordi & Co., Milan.

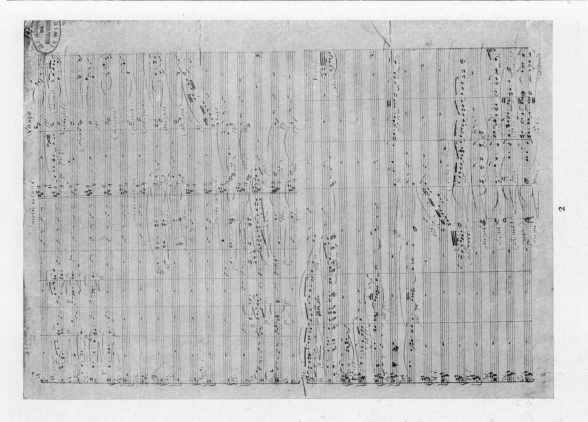

(1) Wagner's friend Mathilde Wesendonck (1828–1902) with her little son Guido, who died young. Chalk drawing by Ernst Benedikt Kietz in 1856. Los Angeles, U.S.A., Collection of P. Max Kuenrich. (2) The close of the Prelude to *Tristan und Isolde* adapted for concert performance. The score, in Wagner's own hand, Vienna, 1861. Bequeathed by Brahms. Vienna, Museum der Gesellschaft der Musikfreunde.

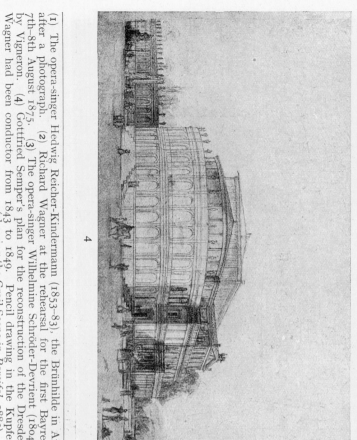

(1) The opera-singer Hedwig Reicher-Kindermann (1853–83), the Brünhilde in Angelo Neumann's travelling Wagner Theatre. Steel engraving by A. Weger, after a photograph.   (2) Richard Wagner at the rehearsal for the first Bayreuth Festival performances. Pencil drawing by Adolph Menzel, Bayreuth, 7th–8th August 1875.   (3) The opera-singer Wilhelmine Schröder-Devrient (1804–60), engaged at the Hoftheater, Dresden, from 1823 to 1847. Lithograph by Vigneron.   (4) Gottfried Semper's plan for the reconstruction of the Dresden Hoftheater. At the old theatre (opened in 1841 and burnt down in 1869) Wagner had been conductor from 1843 to 1849. Pencil drawing in the Kupferstichkabinet, Dresden.   (5) Interior view of the Bayreuth Festival Theatre (showing the Grail Scene in *Parsifal*, 1882).   Photograph by Hans Brand, Bayreuth.

Figs. (1) to (6) Wagner singers: (1) Joseph Tichatschek (1807–86), the first Rienzi and Tannhäuser (Dresden, 1842, 1845). Lithograph by F. Hanfstaengl, 1842. (2) Ludwig Schnorr von Carolsfeld (1836–65), the first Tristan (Munich, 1865). Munich photograph, 1865. (3) Albert Niemann (1831–1917), the first Siegmund of the Bayreuth Festivals (1876). Photograph. (4) Franz Betz (1835–1900), the first Hans Sachs (Munich, 1868) and the first Wotan at Bayreuth (1876). Steel engraving by A. Weger from a photograph. (5) Hermann Winkelmann (1849–1912), as Parsifal in the original performance at Bayreuth, 1882. Photograph. (6) Georg Unger (1837–87), the first Siegfried of the Bayreuth Festivals (1876). Steel engraving by A. Weger, from a photograph. Figs. (7) to (9): Wagner conductors: Hans von Bülow (see fig. 4, p. 327). (7) Hermann Levi (1839–1900), Hofkapellmeister in Carlsruhe and Munich. Conducted the first performance of *Parsifal* in 1882 at Bayreuth. Oil portrait by Franz von Lenbach. Photograph by Bruckmann. (8) Hans Richter (1843–1916), conductor of the first Bayreuth Festival in 1876. Photograph. (9) Siegfried Wagner (b. 1869), son of the master, opera composer and conductor.

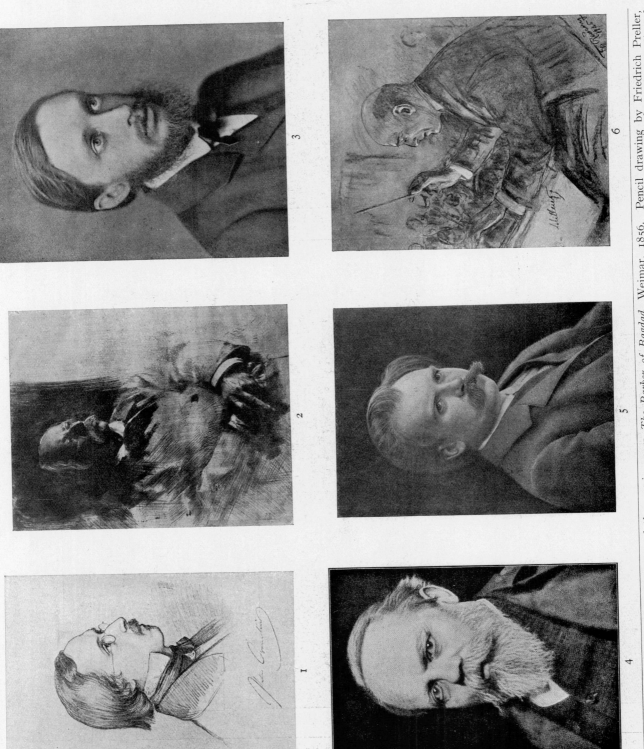

(1) Peter Cornelius (1824–74), composer of the comic opera *The Barber of Bagdad*, Weimar, 1856. Pencil drawing by Friedrich Preller, senior, Weimar, 1856. (2) Karl Goldmark (1830–1915), composer of the opera *The Queen of Sheba*, Vienna, 1875. Etching by Ferdinand Schmutzer (d. 1928). (3) Hermann Goetz (1840–76), composer of the comic opera *Der Widerspenstigen Zähmung* (*The Taming of the Shrew*), Mannheim, 1874. Photograph. (4) Engelbert Humperdinck (1854–1921), composer of the fairy opera *Hänsel und Gretel*, Weimar, 1893. Photograph. (5) Eugen d'Albert (b. 1864), piano virtuoso and composer of the opera *Tiefland*, Prague, 1903. Photograph by G. Brokesch, Leipzig. graph. (6) Max Schillings (b. 1868), composer of the opera *Mona Lisa*, Stuttgart, 1915. Charcoal drawing by Fritz Reusing, 1925.

Danish composers: (1) Christoph Ernst Friedrich Weyse (1774–1842), master of J. P. E. Hartmann and N. W. Gade. Lithograph by Fortling. (2) Friedrich Kuhlau (1786–1832). Unsigned lithograph. (3) Johann Peter Emil Hartmann (1805–1900). Lithograph by J. W. Tegner, from a daguerreotype. (4) Niels Wilhelm Gade (1817–90). Lithograph by Joseph Kriehuber, Vienna, 1844. (5) Jenny Lind (by marriage Gold-schmidt), celebrated as the 'Swedish Nightingale' (1820–87), singing Mendelssohn's song: *Bei der Wiege*. Oil painting by Louis Asher in the National Museum, Stockholm. (6) Edvard Grieg (1843–1907), Norway's most famous composer. Photograph by Fritz Reinhardt (formerly Perscheid) of Leipzig.

1   2   3   4   5   6   7   8

(1) Michael Kelly (1762–1826), a friend of Mozart; opera singer and dramatic composer. Mezzotint by C. Turner, after J. Lonsdale, London, 1825. (2) Michael William Balfe (1808–70), composer of the opera *The Bohemian Girl* (London, 1843). Oil portrait by Rothwell in the National Portrait Gallery, London. Museum photograph. (3) Sir William Sterndale Bennett (1816–75), one of the best English composers of the nineteenth century. Lithograph by C. Baugniet. (4) Sir Michael Costa (1808–84), composer and well-known conductor. Unsigned lithograph. (5) William Vincent Wallace (1818–65), opera composer and pianist. Lithograph by C. Baugniet, London, 1846. (6) Sir Arthur Sullivan (1842–1900), composer of the comic opera *The Mikado* (London, 1885). Photograph by Elliott & Fry, London. (7) Sir Edward Elgar (1857–9134), the most famous English composer of his day. Photograph. (8) Edward MacDowell (1861–1908), the most prominent composer in the United States. Photograph.

1

2

3

(**1**) Friedrich Smetana (1824–84), composer of the comic opera *Prodaná nevěsta* (*The Bartered Bride*) (Prague, 1866). Etching by Johann Lindner. (**2**) Anton Dvořák (1841–1904), the most famous Czech national composer of the immediate past. Etching. (**3**) The Bohemian Quartet, founded in 1892: Karl Hoffmann (b. 1872, first violin), the composer Joseph Suk (b. 1874, second violin), Georg Herold (viola), Hans Wihan (1855–1920, violoncello). Pencil caricature by Hugo Böttinger, 1907.

1   2   3

4   5

(1) Alexis Lvov (1799–1871), author of the Russian National Hymn (1833). Lithograph from the portrait by Franz Krüger. (2) Anton Rubinstein (1829–94), piano virtuoso and composer of the opera *The Demon* (St. Petersburg, 1875). Portrait as a child. Pencil drawing by R. Saletz (?); Dresden, 28th December, 1842. Formerly in the Heyer Museum, Cologne. (3) Alexander Borodin (1833–87), composer of the opera *Prince Igor*. Photograph from the 1880 period. (4) Modeste Mussorgsky (1835–81), composer of the opera *Boris Godunov* (St. Petersburg, 1874). Oil painting by Ilia Repin (1881) in the Tretiakov Gallery, Moscow. (5) Peter Tchaikovsky (1840–93), most prominent Russian composer of the nineteenth century. Oil portrait by Nicolai Kusnezoff (1893) in the Tretiakov Gallery, Moscow.

1

2

3

4

(1) Michael Glinka (1804–57), composer of the opera *A Life for the Tsar* (St. Petersburg, 1836). Pencil drawing by Ilia Repin, 1892: study for the oil painting in the Tretiakov Gallery, Moscow. (2) César Cui (1835–1917). Pencil drawing by Repin, 1892. (3) Mili Balakirev (1837–1910), leader of the so-called new Russian school. Pencil drawing by Repin, 1870. (4) Nicolai Rimsky - Korsakov (1844 – 1908), composer of the national opera *Sadko* (Moscow, 1897). Pencil drawing by Repin, 1888.

(1) Arrigo Boito (1842–1918), composer of the opera *Mefistofele* (Milan, 1868; Bologna, 1875) and librettist for Verdi's operas, *Otello* (Milan, 1887) and *Falstaff* (Milan, 1892).   Photograph.   (2) Amilcare Ponchielli (1834–86), composer of the opera *Gioconda* (Milan, 1876) libretto also by A. Boito).   Photograph.   (3) Ermanno Wolf-Ferrari (b. 1876), composer of the comic opera, *Le donne curiose* (Munich, 1903) (? and the operas, *Le gioielli della Madonna* and *Sly*).   Photograph.   (4) Alberto Franchetti (b. 1860), composer of the opera, *Germania* (Milan, 1902).   Photograph by A. Badodi, Milan.   (5) Francesco Cilea (b. 1866), composer of the opera, *Adrienne Lecouvreur* (Milan, 1902).   Photograph by A. Badodi, Milan.   (6) Arturo Toscanini (b. 1886), conductor; hitherto artistic director of the Teatro alla Scala, Milan.   Drawing by G. Tabet, Milan.

The 'Verismo' school: (**1**) Ruggiero Leoncavallo (1858–1919), composer of the opera *Pagliacci* (Milan, 1892). Photograph. (**2**) Pietro Mascagni (b. 1863), composer of the opera *Cavalleria Rusticana* (Rome, 1890). Photograph by Calzolari, Milan (*c.* 1895). (**3**) Umberto Giordano (*b.* 1867), composer of the opera *Fedora* (Milan, 1898). Photograph by M. Castagneri, Milan. (**4**) Giacomo Puccini (1858–1924), composer of the opera *La Bohème* (Turin, 1896). Photograph by G. Ballerini & Co., Florence. Great Italian singers: (**5**) The baritone Mattia Battistini (1857–1928). Photograph by Montabone, Rome, 1888. (**6**) The tenor Enrico Caruso (1873–1921). Self-portrait (pen-and-ink caricature). Prague, May, 1904. Cologne, Collection of G. Kinsky.

1

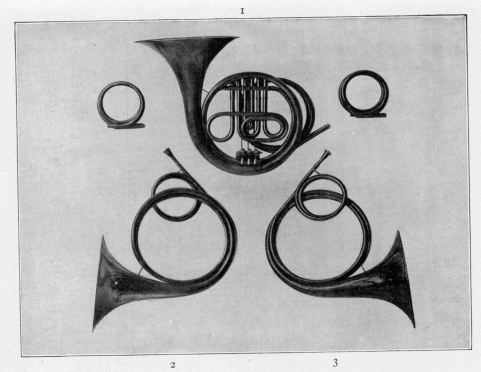

2   3

4   5   6

Brass wind instruments (the horn and trumpet family). (1) to (3) Valvehorn in F (with 3 valves and 2 crooks) and two valveless natural horns by Joseph Riedel, Vienna, (c. 1850). (4) Valve trumpet in F (with 3 Viennese double-valves) by L. Uhlmann, Vienna (c. 1850). The essential progress in the development of the modern orchestra rests upon the invention of the valve (by the Silesian horn-player, Friedrich Blümel in 1813), which enabled horns and trumpets to play the full chromatic scale. (5) Bass ophicleide in brass (a bass keyed horn, forerunner of the bass tuba, invented by Halary of Paris in 1817). Nuremberg, Germanic Museum. (6) Wagner tuba (tenor tuba in B-flat with 4 valves, a tenor horn with waldhorn mouthpiece) by Florian Slack, Vienna (d. 1918), for which Wagner wrote in the *Ring* and Bruckner in his symphonies. Figs. 1 to 4 and 6: Vienna, Art History Museum.

INDEX TO INSTRUMENTS &c.

*